THE KINGFISHER
First
Picture Atlas

Written by Deborah Chancellor

Illustrated by Anthony Lewis

KINGFISHER

KINGFISHER

Kingfisher Publications Plc
New Penderel House
283–288 High Holborn
London WC1V 7HZ

www.kingfisherpub.com

Author: Deborah Chancellor
Senior editor: Belinda Weber
Art director: Mike Davis
Consultant: Keith Lye
DTP Manager: Nicky Studdart
Senior production controller: Lindsey Scott
Picture research manager: Cee Weston-Baker
Proof-reader: Sheila Clewley
Cover design: Mike Davis, Jane Tassie

Illustrations by Anthony Lewis

First published by Kingfisher
Publications Plc 2005

10 9 8 7 6 5 4 3 2 1

1TR/0305/SHENS/CLSN(CLSN)/128MA/C

Copyright © Kingfisher
Publications Plc 2005

A CIP catalogue record for this book
is available from the British Library.

ISBN-13: 978 0 7534 1112 4
ISBN-10: 0 7534 1112 1

Printed in Taiwan

Contents

CREDITS
The Publisher would like to thank the following for permission
to reproduce their material. Every care has been taken to trace copyright
holders. However, if there have been unintentional omissions or failure to
trace copyright holders, we apologise and will, if informed, endeavour to
make corrections in any future edition.

2 NASA; 7 Corbis/Galen Rowell; 8 Corbis/Yann Arthus-Bertrand; 13
Photolibrary/Walter Bibikow; 15 Alamy/Robert Harding Picture Library;
16 Alamy/Bob Turner; 19 Alamy/ Robert Harding Picture Library; 20
Alamy/Imagestate; 22 Alamy/Andre Jenny; 24 Alamy/Mervyn Rees; 27
Corbis/ Reuters; 28 Getty/311214-001; 30 Corbis/Arko Datta/Reuters;
32 Alamy/SC Photos; 35 Alamy/Worldwide Pic Lib; 37 Photolibrary/John
Downer; 38 Corbis/Yann Arthus-Bertrand; 41 Alamy/Robert Harding
Picture Library; 42 Rex; 43 Getty/Stone; 45 Alamy/Nordicphotos

About the earth

The earth is a planet in space. It is shaped like a ball and is covered with land and sea. Photographs can show us what the earth looks like. Maps help us understand more about the world.

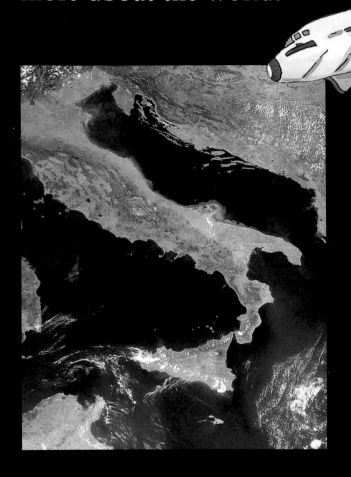

Countries of the world

A country (such as Italy, map above) is a part of the world with its own people and laws. There are over 200 countries in the world. The number changes if countries break up or join together in new ways.

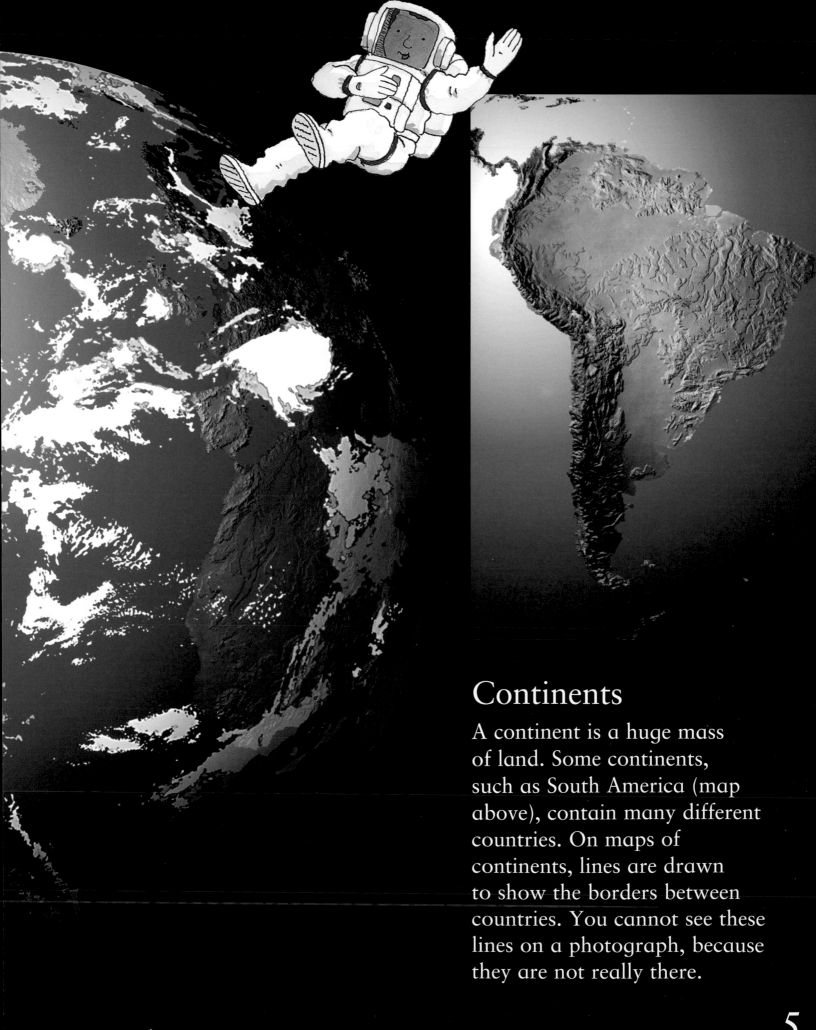

Continents

A continent is a huge mass of land. Some continents, such as South America (map above), contain many different countries. On maps of continents, lines are drawn to show the borders between countries. You cannot see these lines on a photograph, because they are not really there.

What is a map?

A map is a picture of the earth that shows natural and man-made features. A globe is a kind of map that is in the shape of a ball, just like the earth itself. We cannot see the whole world at once on a globe. If we want to do this, we need to look at a flat map.

Making a map

To make a flat map, the globe is split into segments, and 'peeled' like an orange.

The segments are then placed side by side.

These segments are used to create a flat map (see the map of the world on page 10).

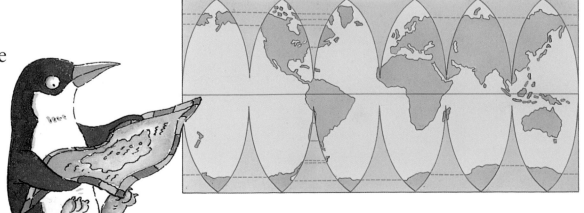

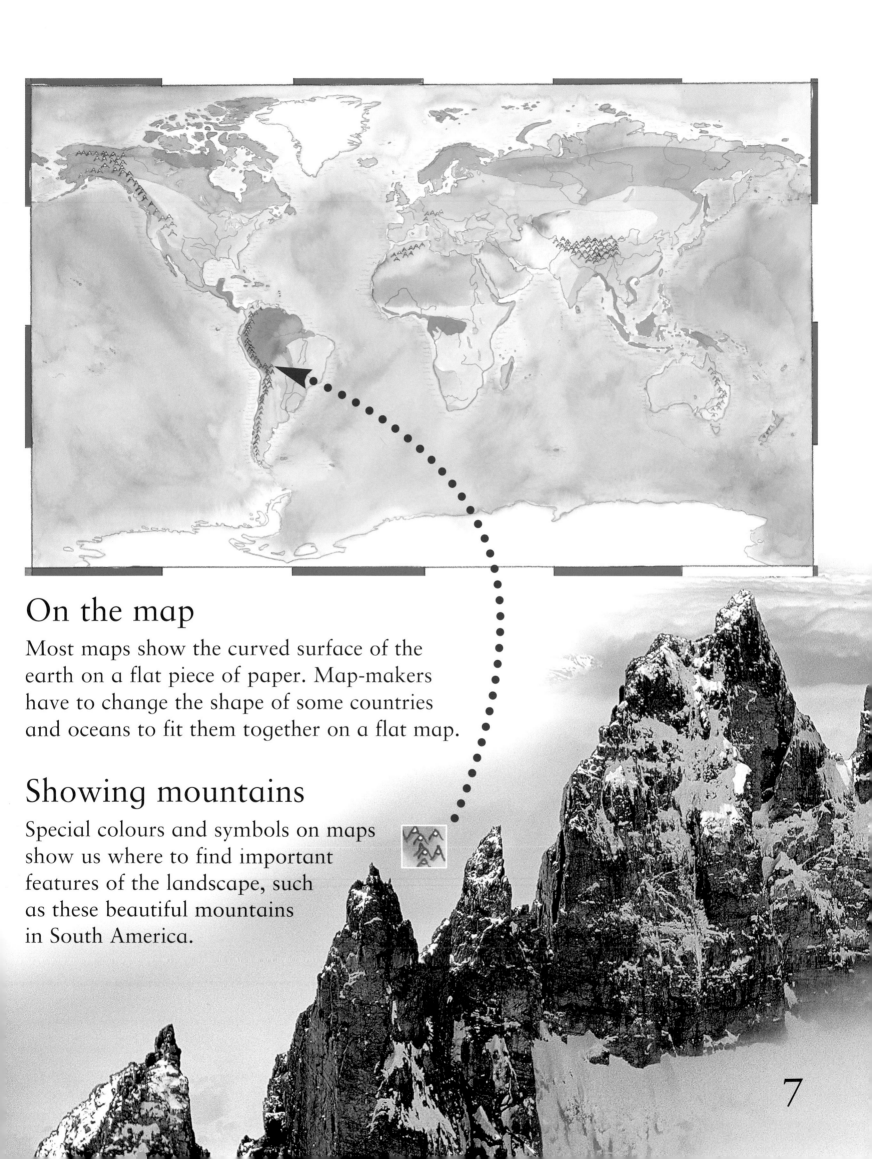

On the map

Most maps show the curved surface of the earth on a flat piece of paper. Map-makers have to change the shape of some countries and oceans to fit them together on a flat map.

Showing mountains

Special colours and symbols on maps show us where to find important features of the landscape, such as these beautiful mountains in South America.

7

Using an atlas

An atlas is a book of maps. To use an atlas, you need to understand how maps work. Maps are much smaller than the places they show. They have lots of information in a very small space.

Pictures show industries, animals or landmarks.

Grid band 'C'

A small world map shows you where to find the countries shown on the main map.

Grid band '2'

A grid helps you find places on the map. Here, Alice Springs is in square C2. You can find this by tracing your finger down from the letter C band and across from the number 2 band.

In this atlas, a story box picks out an interesting fact.

A	B	C

Darwin

Seahorse

Gulf of Carpentaria

Aboriginal cave painting

NORTHERN TERRITORY

Great Sandy Desert

A U S T R A L I

TROPIC OF CAPRICORN

Mining

Gibson Desert

WESTERN AUSTRALIA

Kangaroo

Great Victoria Desert

Alice Springs

Simpson Desert

SOUTH AUSTRALIA

Lake Eyre

The Ghan

Perth

Farming

Great Australian Bight

Adelaide

Great white shark

Uluru is a sandstone monolith rising high above the desert in Australia's Northern Territory. It is the largest rock of its kind in the world.

Look for the star ✸

38

A	B	C

8

Map key

Colours, lines and symbols on maps stand for many different things. These details are explained in a key to the map. In this atlas, the key helps you find cities, borders and rivers. It also shows what the colours on the map mean.

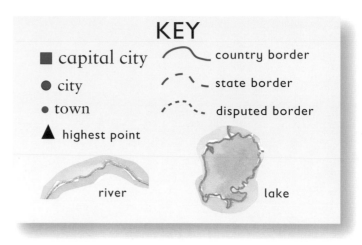

KEY
- ■ capital city
- ● city
- • town
- ▲ highest point
- ⌒ country border
- - - state border
- - - - disputed border
- river
- lake

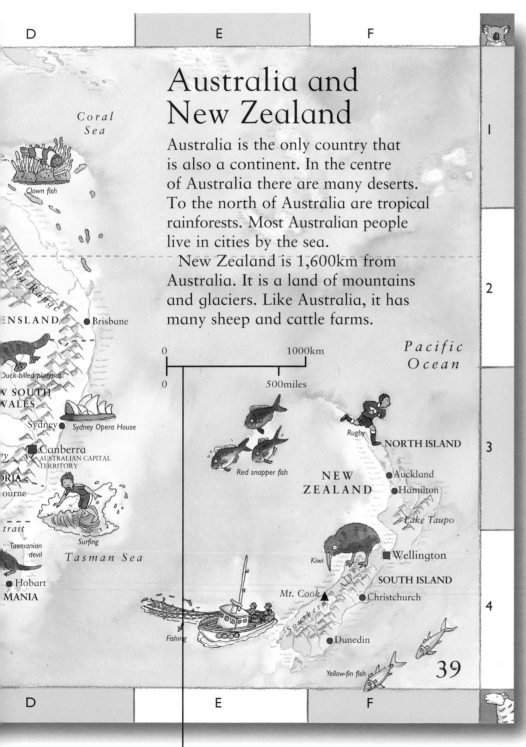

Australia and New Zealand

Australia is the only country that is also a continent. In the centre of Australia there are many deserts. To the north of Australia are tropical rainforests. Most Australian people live in cities by the sea.

New Zealand is 1,600km from Australia. It is a land of mountains and glaciers. Like Australia, it has many sheep and cattle farms.

0   1000km
0   500miles

Coral Sea
Clown fish
Duck-billed platypus
ENSLAND • Brisbane
W SOUTH VALES
Sydney • Sydney Opera House
■ Canberra
AUSTRALIAN CAPITAL TERRITORY
ORIA
ourne
Surfing
trait
Tasmanian devil
Tasman Sea
• Hobart
MANIA
Fishing
Red snapper fish
Rugby
NORTH ISLAND
NEW ZEALAND
● Auckland
● Hamilton
Lake Taupo
Kiwi
■ Wellington
SOUTH ISLAND
Mt. Cook ▲
● Christchurch
● Dunedin
Yellow-fin fish
Pacific Ocean

39

Desert Dry areas with sand and rocks

Dry grassland Flat, grassy plains with only a few trees

Temperate grassland Flat, grassy plains with some trees

Forest Areas with lots of trees

Mountains Tall hills and rugged landscape

Tundra Flat area near Arctic with frozen ground and no trees

Ice and snow Places where ice and snow cover the ground

Seas and oceans Salty water that covers much of the earth

A scale bar helps you understand how big areas are on the map.

9

1

NORTH
AMERICA

*Atlantic
Ocean*

2

*Pacific
Ocean*

SOUTH
AMERICA

The world

3

Maps of the world show the seven
continents. All the continents, except
Antarctica and Australia, are made
up of many different countries.
Lines are drawn on world maps
that do not exist on the ground,
for example the Equator and the
Tropics of Cancer and Capricorn.

*Atlantic
Ocean*

4

10

PRIME
MERIDIAN

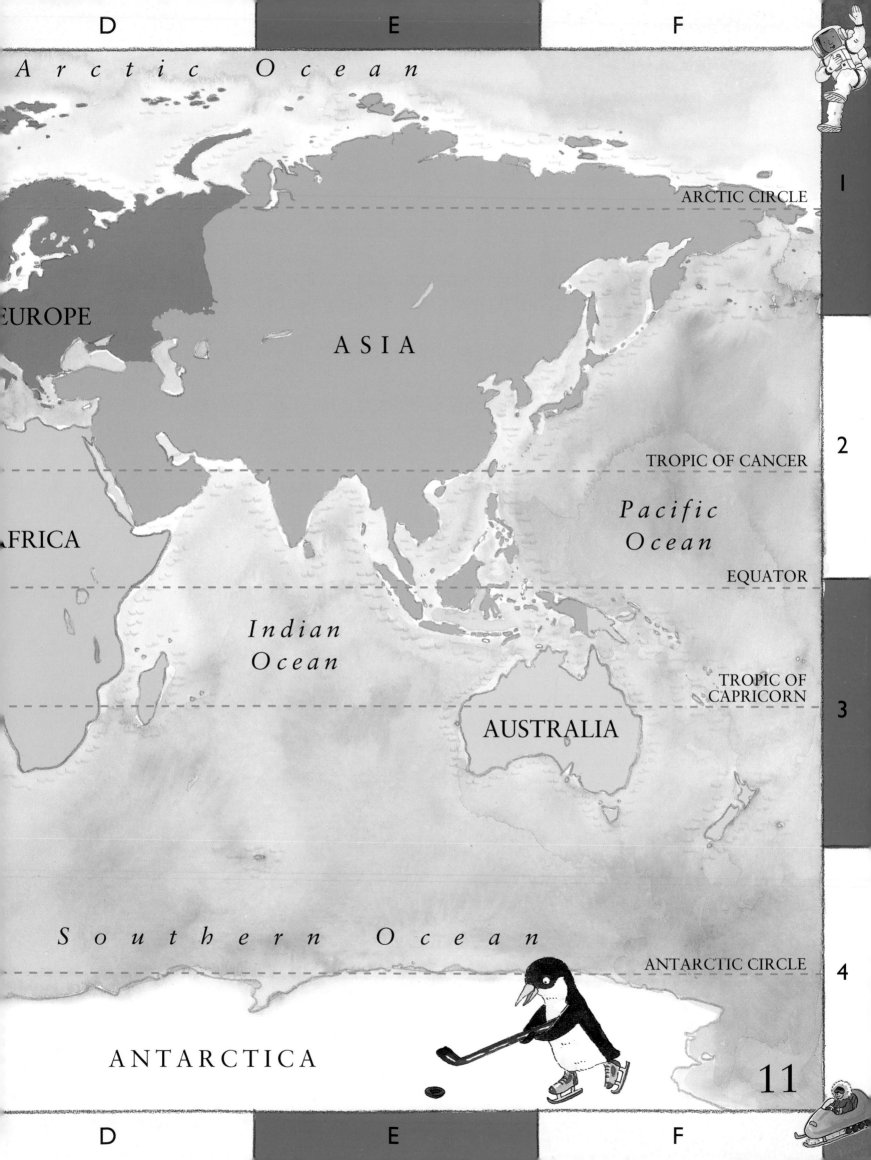

Arctic Ocean

ARCTIC CIRCLE

1

EUROPE

ASIA

TROPIC OF CANCER

2

AFRICA

Pacific
Ocean

EQUATOR

Indian
Ocean

TROPIC OF
CAPRICORN

3

AUSTRALIA

Southern Ocean

ANTARCTIC CIRCLE

4

ANTARCTICA

11

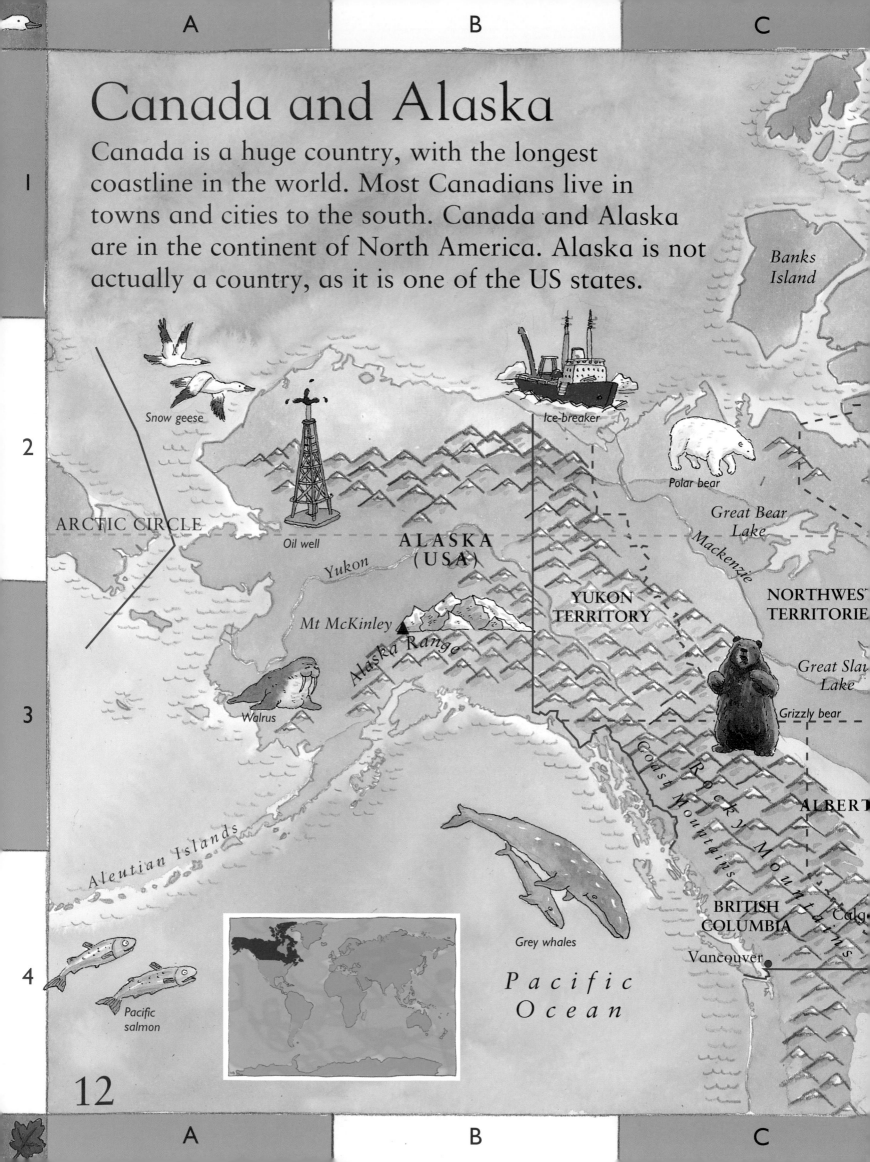

Canada and Alaska

Canada is a huge country, with the longest coastline in the world. Most Canadians live in towns and cities to the south. Canada and Alaska are in the continent of North America. Alaska is not actually a country, as it is one of the US states.

Banks Island

Snow geese

Ice-breaker

Polar bear

Great Bear Lake

Mackenzie

ARCTIC CIRCLE

Oil well

Yukon

ALASKA (USA)

YUKON TERRITORY

NORTHWEST TERRITORIE

Mt McKinley

Alaska Range

Great Sla Lake

Grizzly bear

Walrus

Coast Mountains

Rocky Mountains

ALBERT

Aleutian Islands

Grey whales

BRITISH COLUMBIA

Calg

Pacific salmon

Pacific Ocean

Vancouver

12

ueen Elizabeth Islands

Ellesmere
Island

Devon
Island

Victoria
Island

Baffin
Island

Québec City is the only
walled city in North
America. It was founded
in 1608, and is almost
400 years old.

**Look for
the star** ✵

N U N A V U T

ARCTIC CIRCLE

Reindeer

Inuit

Lake
Athabasca

*H u d s o n
B a y*

Iceberg

MANITOBA

SASKATCHEWAN

*A t l a n t i c
O c e a n*

C A N A D A

Skier

Lake
Winnipeg

Timber industry

QUEBEC

**NEWFOUNDLAND
AND LABRADOR**

Arable farming

ONTARIO

Lake
Superior

Industry

St Lawrence

**NEW
BRUNSWICK**

Toronto's
CN Tower

1000km

Lake
Huron

● Montreal

■ Ottawa

Lake Ontario

**PRINCE
EDWARD
ISLAND**

500miles

Lake Erie

NOVA SCOTIA

13

I

2

3

4

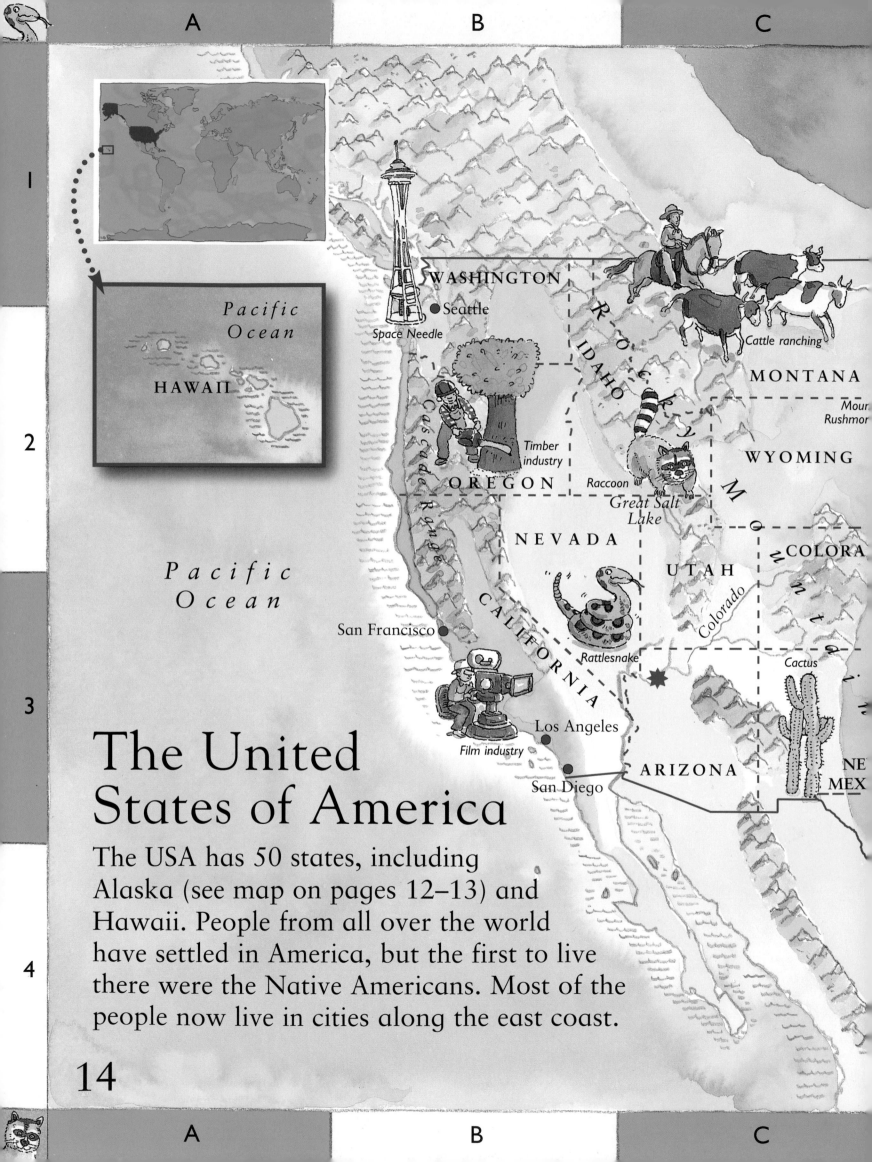

1

2

Pacific Ocean

HAWAII

Pacific Ocean

WASHINGTON

● Seattle

Space Needle

Timber industry

OREGON

Cascade Range

Raccoon

Great Salt Lake

NEVADA

San Francisco ●

CALIFORNIA

Rattlesnake

● Los Angeles

Film industry

● San Diego

ROCKY

IDAHO

Mountains

Cattle ranching

MONTANA

Mour Rushmor

WYOMING

UTAH

Colorado

COLORA

ARIZONA

Cactus

NE
MEX

3

The United States of America

The USA has 50 states, including
Alaska (see map on pages 12–13) and
Hawaii. People from all over the world
have settled in America, but the first to live
there were the Native Americans. Most of the
people now live in cities along the east coast.

4

14

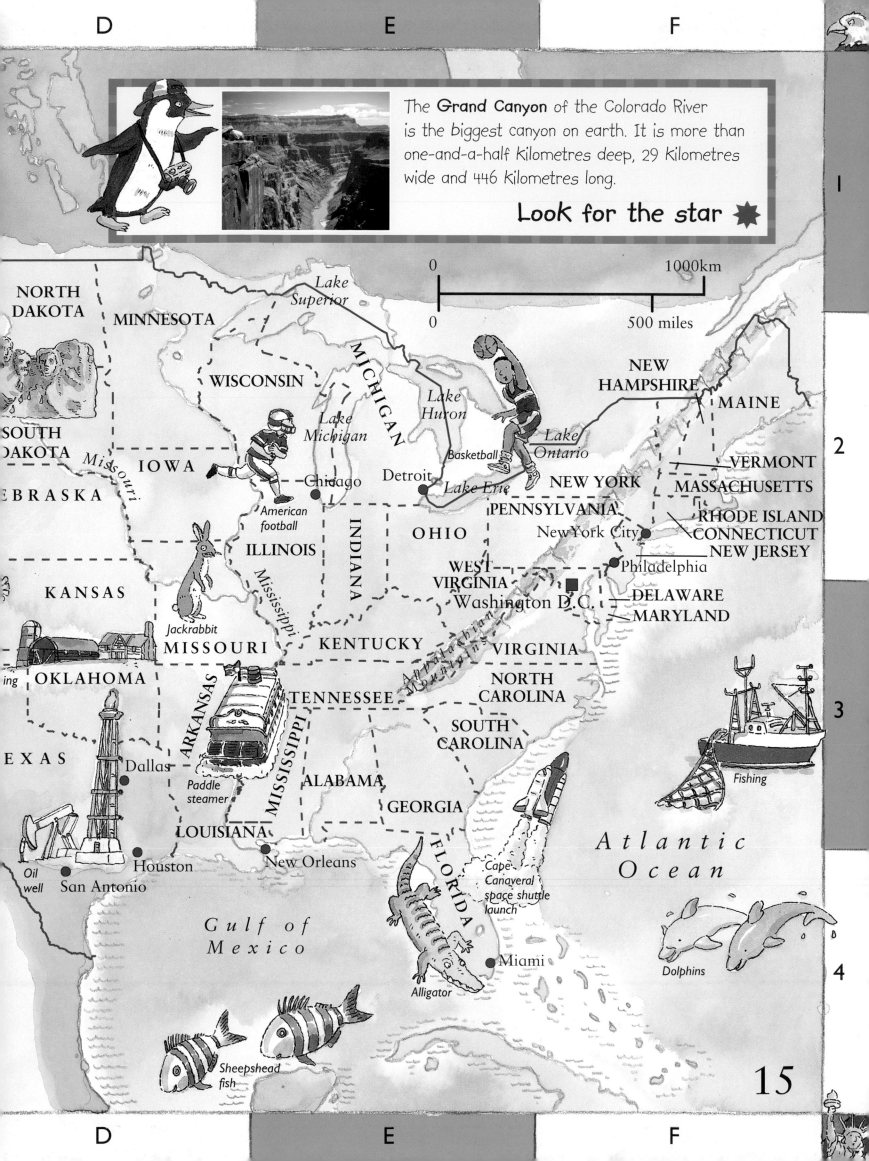

The **Grand Canyon** of the Colorado River is the biggest canyon on earth. It is more than one-and-a-half kilometres deep, 29 kilometres wide and 446 kilometres long.

Look for the star ✴

0   1000km

0   500 miles

NORTH DAKOTA

MINNESOTA

SOUTH DAKOTA

WISCONSIN

Lake Superior

MICHIGAN

Lake Huron

Lake Michigan

Lake Ontario

NEW HAMPSHIRE

MAINE

VERMONT

Basketball

MASSACHUSETTS

Missouri

IOWA

Chicago

Detroit

Lake Erie

NEW YORK

NEBRASKA

American football

ILLINOIS

INDIANA

OHIO

PENNSYLVANIA

New York City

RHODE ISLAND

CONNECTICUT

NEW JERSEY

Jackrabbit

Mississippi

WEST VIRGINIA

Philadelphia

KANSAS

Washington D.C.

DELAWARE

MARYLAND

ing

OKLAHOMA

MISSOURI

KENTUCKY

VIRGINIA

ARKANSAS

TENNESSEE

NORTH CAROLINA

SOUTH CAROLINA

Appalachian Mountains

Fishing

TEXAS

Dallas

Paddle steamer

MISSISSIPPI

ALABAMA

GEORGIA

Oil well

Houston

San Antonio

LOUISIANA

New Orleans

FLORIDA

Cape Canaveral space shuttle launch

Atlantic Ocean

Gulf of Mexico

Alligator

Miami

Dolphins

Sheepshead fish

D   E   F

1

2

3

4

15

1

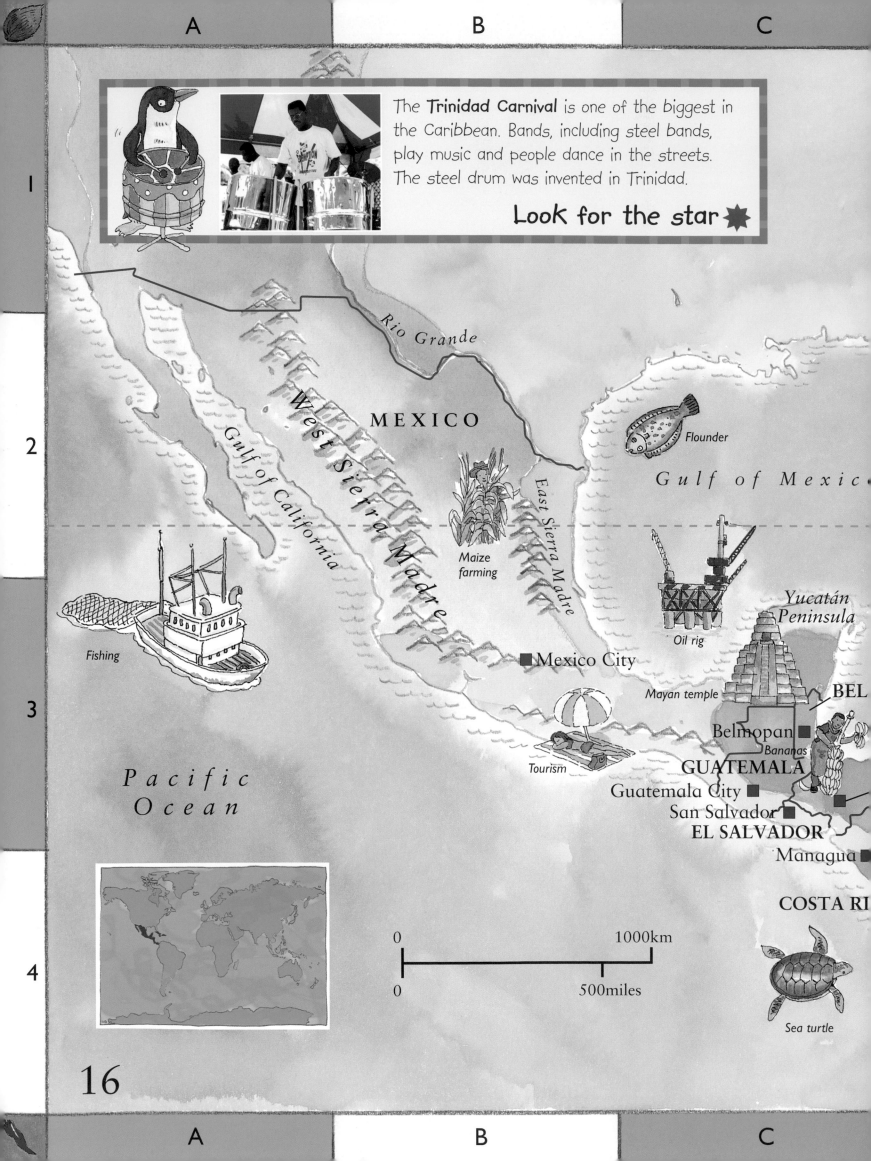

The **Trinidad Carnival** is one of the biggest in the Caribbean. Bands, including steel bands, play music and people dance in the streets. The steel drum was invented in Trinidad.

Look for the star ✴

Rio Grande

MEXICO

2

Gulf of California

West Sierra Madre

East Sierra Madre

Flounder

Gulf of Mexic

Maize farming

Oil rig

Yucatán Peninsula

Fishing

3

■ Mexico City

Mayan temple

BEL

Belmopan ■

Bananas

GUATEMALA

Guatemala City ■

Tourism

San Salvador ■

EL SALVADOR

P a c i f i c
O c e a n

Managua ■

COSTA RI

```
0                    1000km
|————————————————————|
0                    500miles
```

4

Sea turtle

16

Mexico, Central America and the Caribbean

Mexico, Central America and the Caribbean islands are in the continent of North America. Mexico is the largest country in the region. The islands of the Caribbean are countries too. More than half of all Caribbean people live in Cuba and the Dominican Republic.

Palm tree

BAHAMAS
■ Nassau

TROPIC OF CANCER

■ Havana

Coral reef

Scuba diving

Atlantic Ocean

CUBA

Sugar cane

DOMINICAN REPUBLIC

HAITI

PUERTO RICO (USA)
■ San Juan

JAMAICA
■ Kingston

Port-au-Prince

Santo Domingo

ANTIGUA & BARBUDA

ST KITTS & NEVIS

HONDURAS
ucigalpa

Caribbean Sea

DOMINICA
ST LUCIA
ST VINCENT & THE GRENADINES
BARBADOS

ARAGUA

GRENADA

Spotfin butterfly fish

■ Port-of-Spain
TRINIDAD & TOBAGO

n José   *Panama Canal*

ANAMA ■ Panama City

17

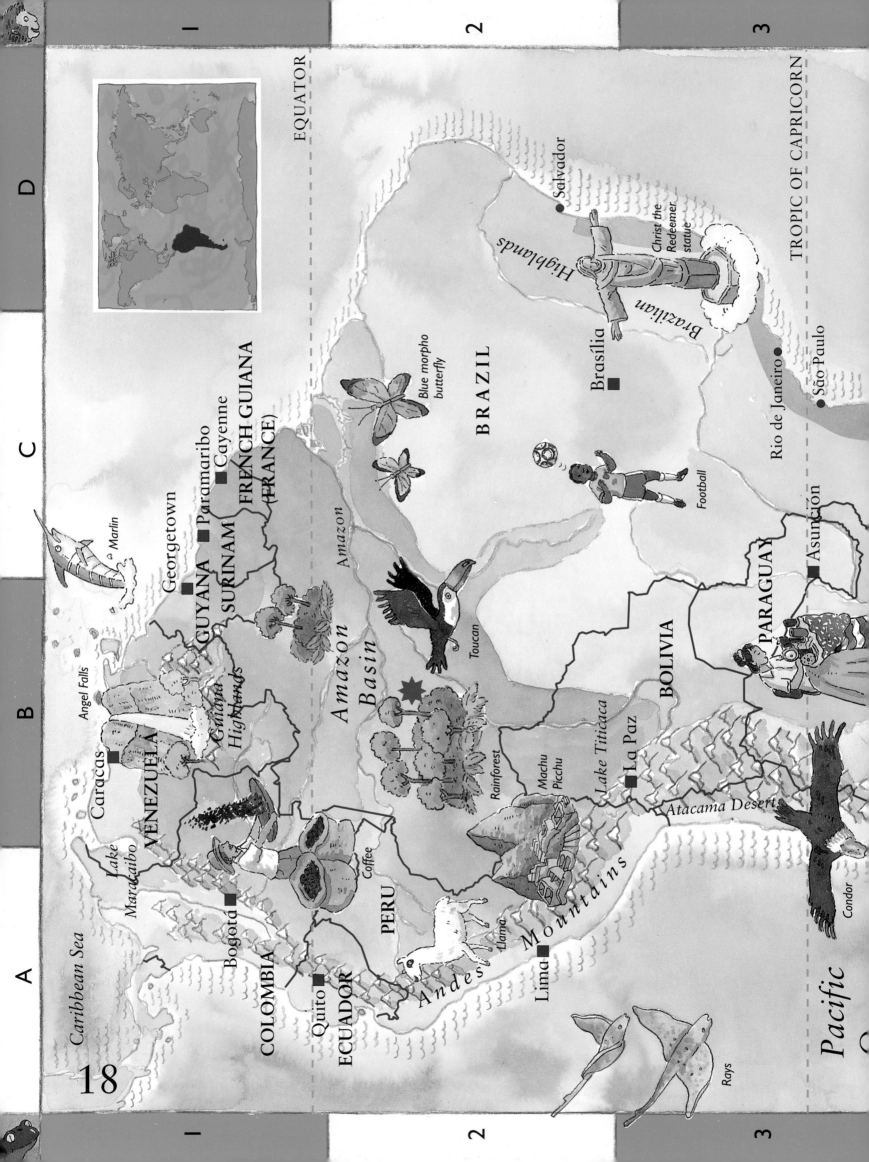

18

A   B   C   D

1   2   3

EQUATOR

TROPIC OF CAPRICORN

Caribbean Sea

Lake Maracaibo

Angel Falls

Marlin

VENEZUELA

Caracas

COLOMBIA

Bogotá

Guiana Highlands

Georgetown

GUYANA

Paramaribo

SURINAM

Cayenne

FRENCH GUIANA (FRANCE)

Quito

ECUADOR

Coffee

PERU

Lima

Llama

Andes Mountains

Amazon Basin

Amazon

Rainforest

Blue morpho butterfly

Toucan

Machu Picchu

Lake Titicaca

La Paz

BOLIVIA

Atacama Desert

Condor

BRAZIL

Brasília

Brazilian Highlands

Christ the Redeemer statue

Salvador

Football

Rio de Janeiro

São Paulo

PARAGUAY

Asunción

Pacific

Rays

South America

South America is a continent of extremes. Tall, snowy mountains lie to the west, while the steamy Amazon rainforest covers a huge area to the north. The southern tip of the continent is very dry and freezing cold.

Aeroplane

0   1000km
0   500miles

The Amazon rainforest contains about half of all the animal and plant species in the world. Many are still waiting to be discovered.

Look for the star ★

URUGUAY
■ Montevideo

Santa Fé ●
Paraná
■ Buenos Aires

ARGENTINA

Sheep farming

FALKLAND ISLANDS (UK)
■ Stanley

Oil rig

Mt Aconcagua ▲
■ Santiago
Andes Mountains

Grapes

Concepción ●
CHILE

Patagonia

Cape Horn

Sardines

Fishing

4   5   6

D   C   B   A

Northern Europe

Forests, lakes and mountains cover large parts of northern Europe. The countries Norway, Sweden and Denmark make up a region called Scandinavia. To the east lies Finland. South of the Baltic Sea are the small countries of Estonia, Latvia and Lithuania.

ARCTIC CIRCLE

ICELAND

Geyser
■ Reykjavik

Cod

Iceland cat shark

Fishing

Atlantic Ocean

Hans Christian Andersen, the famous children's writer, lived in Denmark. A statue of his Little Mermaid is in Copenhagen, the Danish capital city.

Look for the star ✹

Nor
Se

PRIME MERIDIAN 0°

D

E

F

0
400km

0
200miles

Hammerfest

Norwegian Sea

Fjord

L a p l a n d

Kiruna

Arctic fox

Reindeer and Sami

Pine forest

ARCTIC CIRCLE

FINLAND

Oulu

Lake Oulujärvi

SWEDEN

Oil rig

Trondheim

Pine forest

Gulf of Bothnia

Paper mills

L a k e r e g i o n

NORWAY

Bergen

Oslo

Industry

Åland

Stockholm

Baltic Sea

Helsinki

Gulf of Finland

Tallinn

ESTONIA

Lake Vänern

Lake Vättern

Gotland

LATVIA

Gôteborg

Ríga

DENMARK

Pig farming

Cattle farming

Copenhagen

LITHUANIA

Lego

Vilnius

1

2

3

4

21

Western Europe

Much of the land in western Europe is used for farming. Industries, such as car factories, are also important. Some cities are very old, and attract many tourists. Countries around the Mediterranean Sea are very hot in summer.

Atlantic Ocean

Cod

Puffin

Oil rig

North Sea

Windmill

Baltic Sea

Car industry

Tulips

SCOTLAND

Edinburgh

UNITED KINGDOM

NETHERLANDS

NORTHERN IRELAND

Belfast

Dublin

Computers

ENGLAND

France's most famous landmark, the **Eiffel Tower**, sways up to 12cm from side to side in high winds.

Look for the star

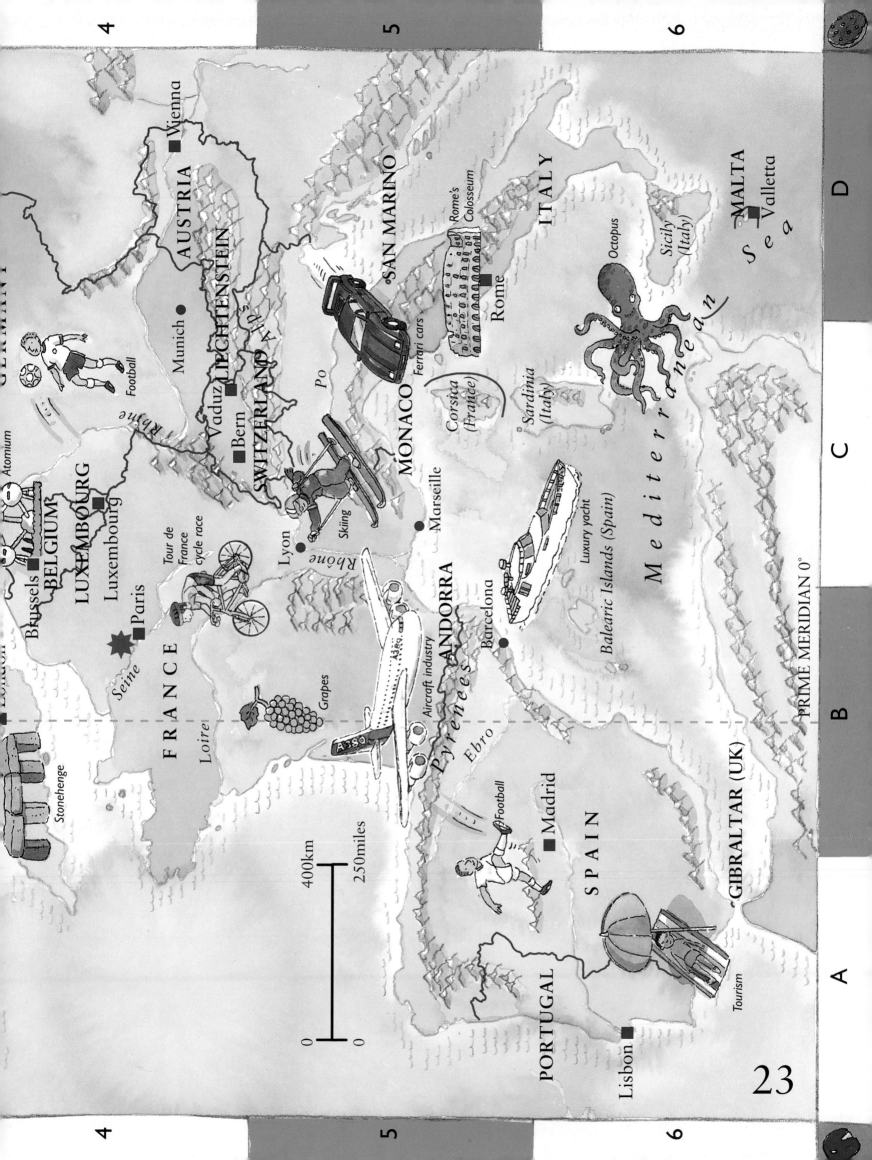

23

GERMANY

Atomium

Brussels
BELGIUM

LUXEMBOURG

Luxembourg

Munich

Football

AUSTRIA

Vaduz LIECHTENSTEIN

Bern

SWITZERLAND

Rhine

Vienna

Stonehenge

Paris

FRANCE

Loire

Seine

Grapes

Tour de
France
cycle race

Po

SAN MARINO

Ferrari cars

Rome's
Colosseum

ITALY

Rome

Octopus

Sicily
(Italy)

MALTA

Valletta

S e a

Aircraft industry

A380

Pyrenees

Ebro

ANDORRA

Barcelona

Skiing

Lyon

Rhône

Marseille

MONACO

Corsica
(France)

Sardinia
(Italy)

M e d i t e r r a n e a n

Luxury yacht

Balearic Islands (Spain)

400km

250miles

0

0

Football

Madrid

S P A I N

Tourism

PORTUGAL

Lisbon

GIBRALTAR (UK)

PRIME MERIDIAN 0°

A   B   C   D

4

5

6

In Kazanlak, Bulgaria, **roses** are an important crop. Valuable oil is taken from their petals to make perfume. As many as 60 roses are needed to produce just one drop of oil.

Look for the star

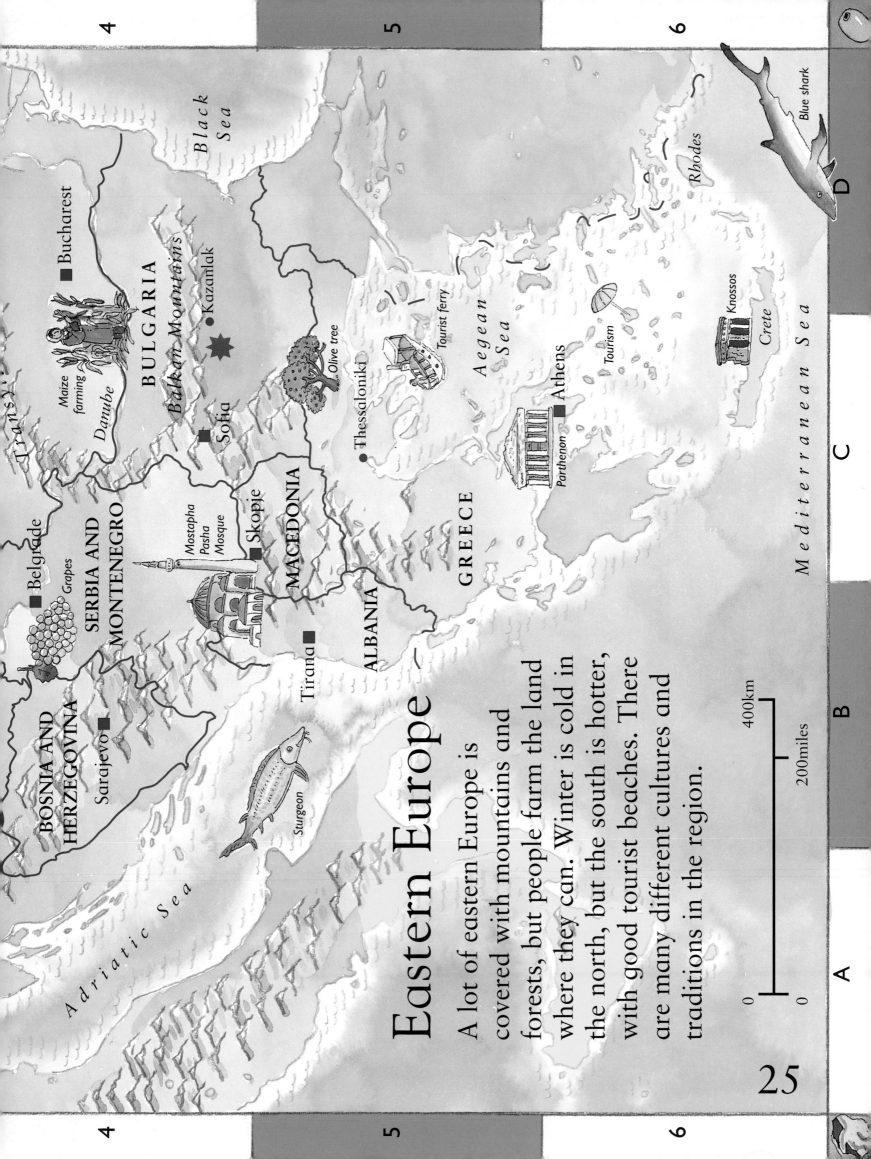

Eastern Europe

A lot of eastern Europe is covered with mountains and forests, but people farm the land where they can. Winter is cold in the north, but the south is hotter, with good tourist beaches. There are many different cultures and traditions in the region.

0
200miles
0
400km

Adriatic Sea

Sturgeon

BOSNIA AND HERZEGOVINA
Sarajevo ■

SERBIA AND MONTENEGRO
Belgrade ■
Grapes

Transylva...

Bucharest ■

Maize farming

BULGARIA
Danube

Balkan Mountains

Sofia ■

Kazanlak

Black Sea

Mostapha Pasha Mosque

Skopje ■
MACEDONIA

Olive tree

Tirana ■
ALBANIA

Thessaloniki

Tourist ferry

GREECE

Aegean Sea

Parthenon
Athens ●

Tourism

Rhodes

Crete
Knossos

Mediterranean Sea

Blue shark

A   B   C   D

4   5   6

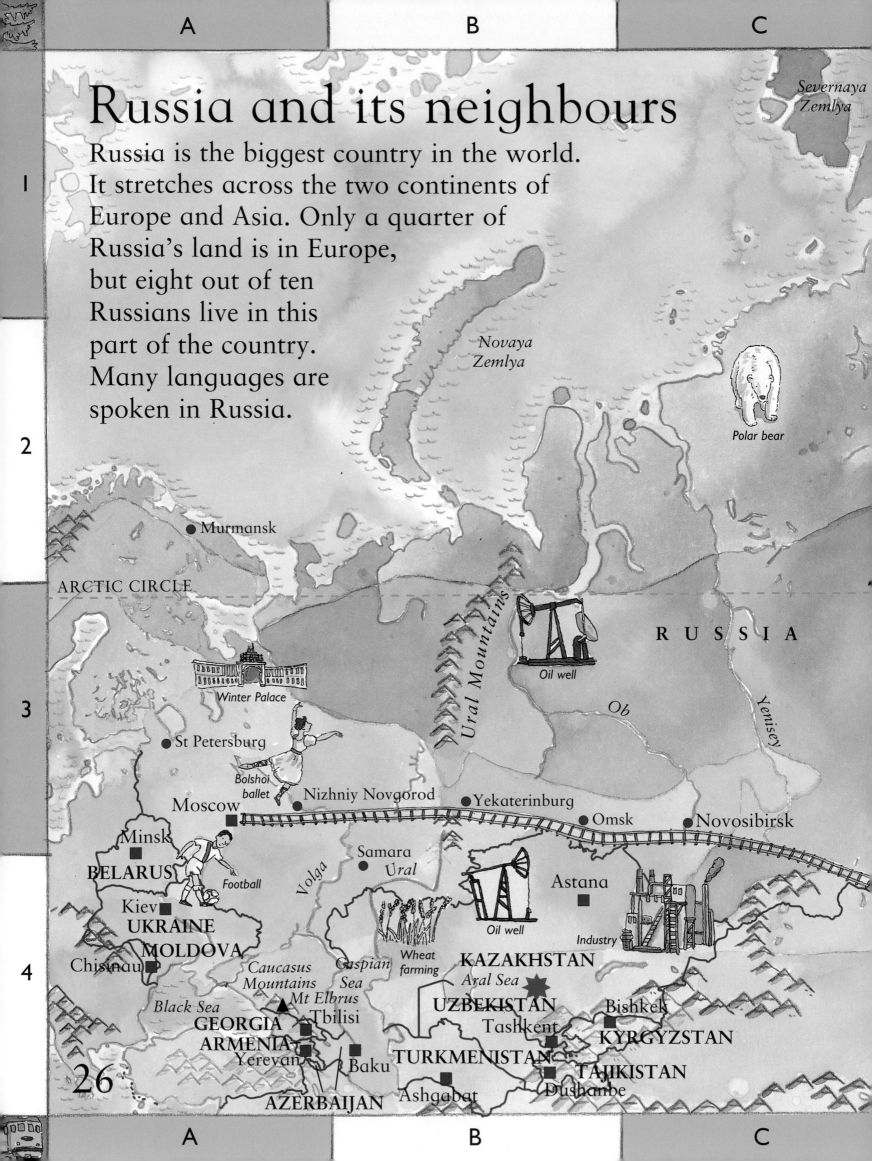

Russia and its neighbours

Russia is the biggest country in the world.
It stretches across the two continents of
Europe and Asia. Only a quarter of
Russia's land is in Europe,
but eight out of ten
Russians live in this
part of the country.
Many languages are
spoken in Russia.

Severnaya Zemlya

Novaya Zemlya

Polar bear

Murmansk

ARCTIC CIRCLE

Ural Mountains

R U S S I A

Oil well

Ob

Yenisey

Winter Palace

St Petersburg

Bolshoi ballet

Moscow

Nizhniy Novgorod

Yekaterinburg

Omsk

Novosibirsk

Minsk

BELARUS

Football

Samara

Ural

Volga

Astana

Oil well

Industry

Kiev

UKRAINE

MOLDOVA

Chisinau

Caucasus Mountains

Caspian Sea

Wheat farming

KAZAKHSTAN

Aral Sea

Black Sea

Mt Elbrus

Tbilisi

UZBEKISTAN

Bishkek

GEORGIA

ARMENIA

Yerevan

Baku

Tashkent

KYRGYZSTAN

TURKMENISTAN

TAJIKISTAN

26

AZERBAIJAN

Ashgabat

Dushanbe

A · B · C

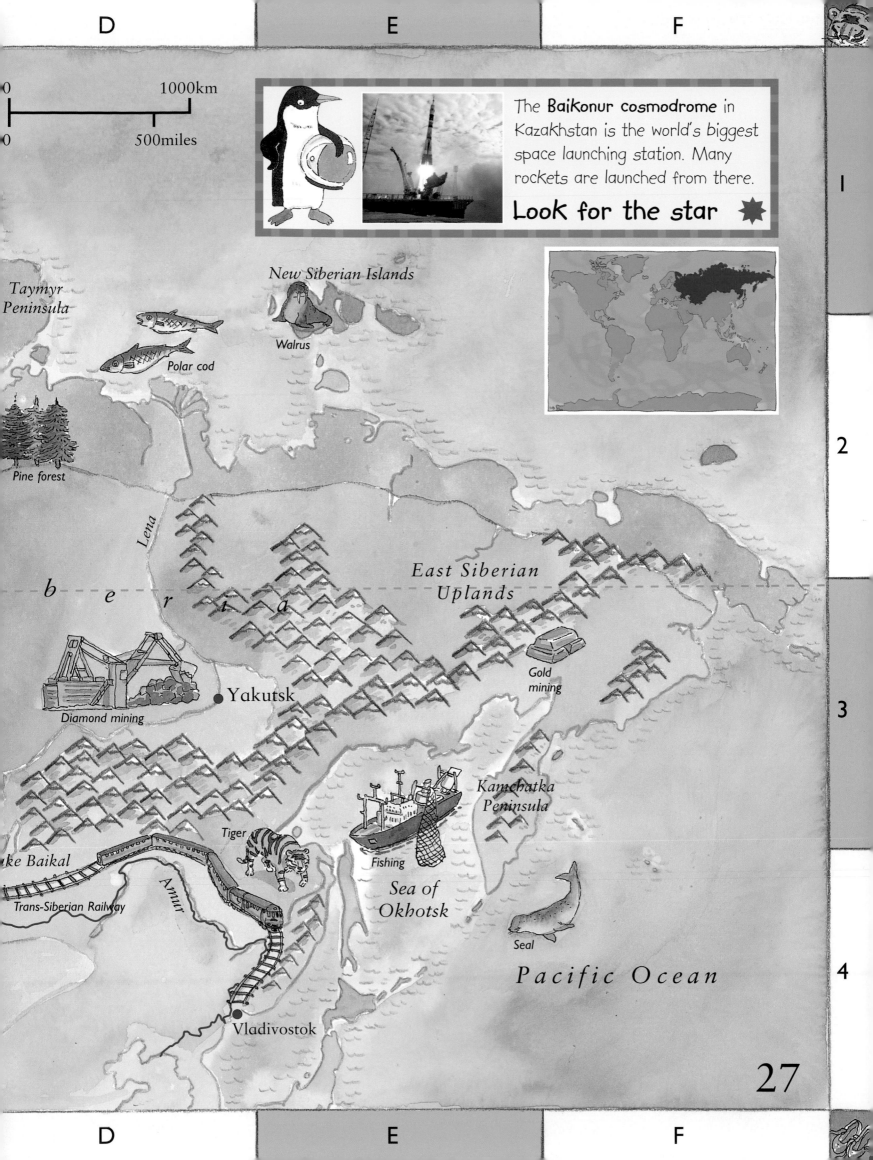

0   1000km

0   500miles

The **Baikonur cosmodrome** in Kazakhstan is the world's biggest space launching station. Many rockets are launched from there.

Look for the star ✦

1

Taymyr Peninsula

New Siberian Islands

Walrus

Polar cod

Pine forest

2

Lena

b   e   r   i   a

East Siberian Uplands

Gold mining

Diamond mining

● Yakutsk

3

Kamchatka Peninsula

ke Baikal

Tiger

Fishing

Trans-Siberian Railway

Amur

Sea of Okhotsk

Seal

Pacific Ocean

4

● Vladivostok

27

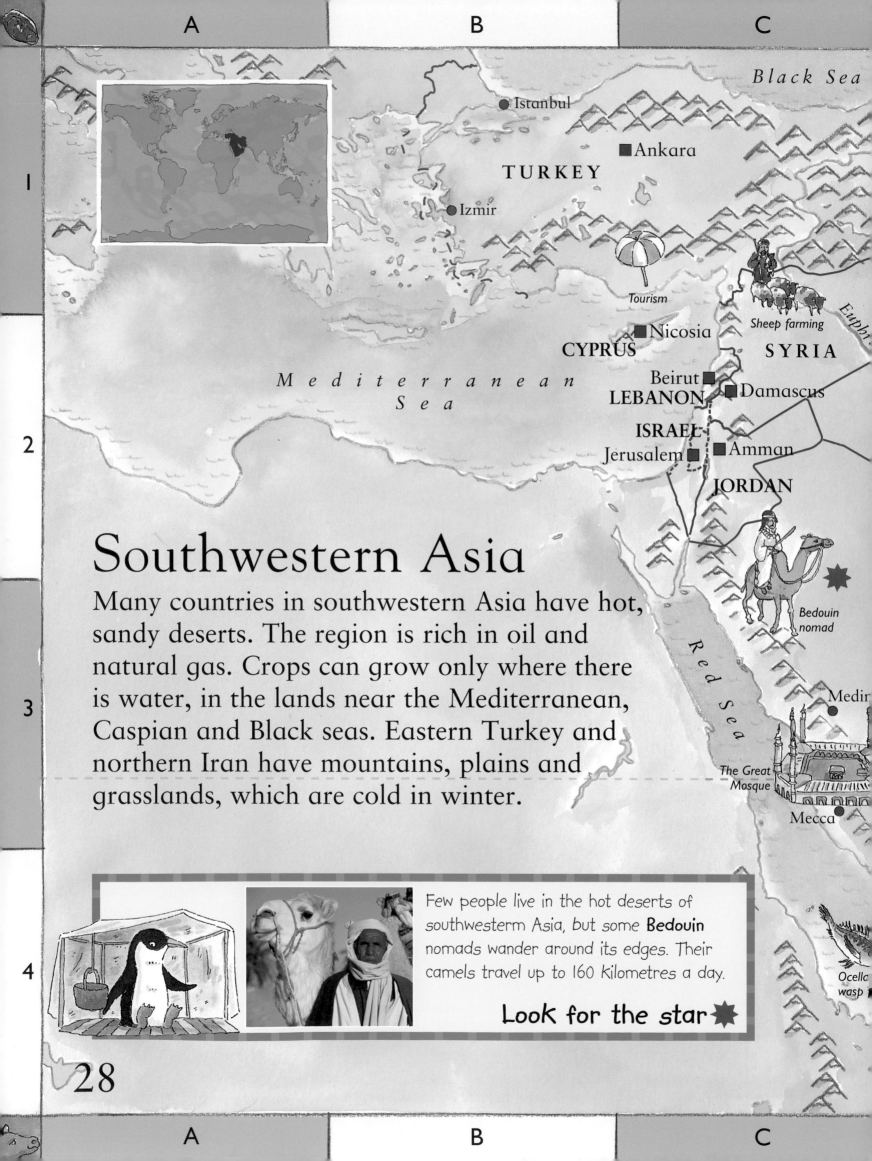

Black Sea

●Istanbul

■Ankara

TURKEY

●Izmir

Tourism

Nicosia■ **SYRIA**

CYPRUS *Sheep farming*

M e d i t e r r a n e a n   S e a

Beirut■

LEBANON Damascus■

ISRAEL

Jerusalem■ ■Amman

JORDAN

Euphr.

Bedouin nomad

Southwestern Asia

Many countries in southwestern Asia have hot, sandy deserts. The region is rich in oil and natural gas. Crops can grow only where there is water, in the lands near the Mediterranean, Caspian and Black seas. Eastern Turkey and northern Iran have mountains, plains and grasslands, which are cold in winter.

Red Sea

●Medir

The Great Mosque

●Mecca

Ocella wasp

Few people live in the hot deserts of southwestern Asia, but some **Bedouin** nomads wander around its edges. Their camels travel up to 160 kilometres a day.

Look for the star ✴

28

0   800km

0   500miles

*Caspian
Sea*

• Tabriz

Oil rig

• Mashhad

Mosul

Tigris

Carpet making

Onager

I R A N

□ Baghdad

IRAQ

• Esfahan

Zagros Mountains

Basra •

KUWAIT

□ Kuwait City

*The
Gulf*

Oil refinery

Oil well

BAHRAIN

□ Manama

OMAN

AUDI ARABIA

QATAR

□ Doha

Oil well

Riyadh □

Abu Dhabi □

U. A. E.

□ Muscat

TROPIC OF CANCER

Arabian Desert

OMAN

*Empty Quarter
(Rub al Khali)*

Dhow

*A r a b i a n
S e a*

YEMEN

Arabian
oryx

Orange-spotted
trevally

□ Sana

Dates

Aden •

Gulf of Aden

29

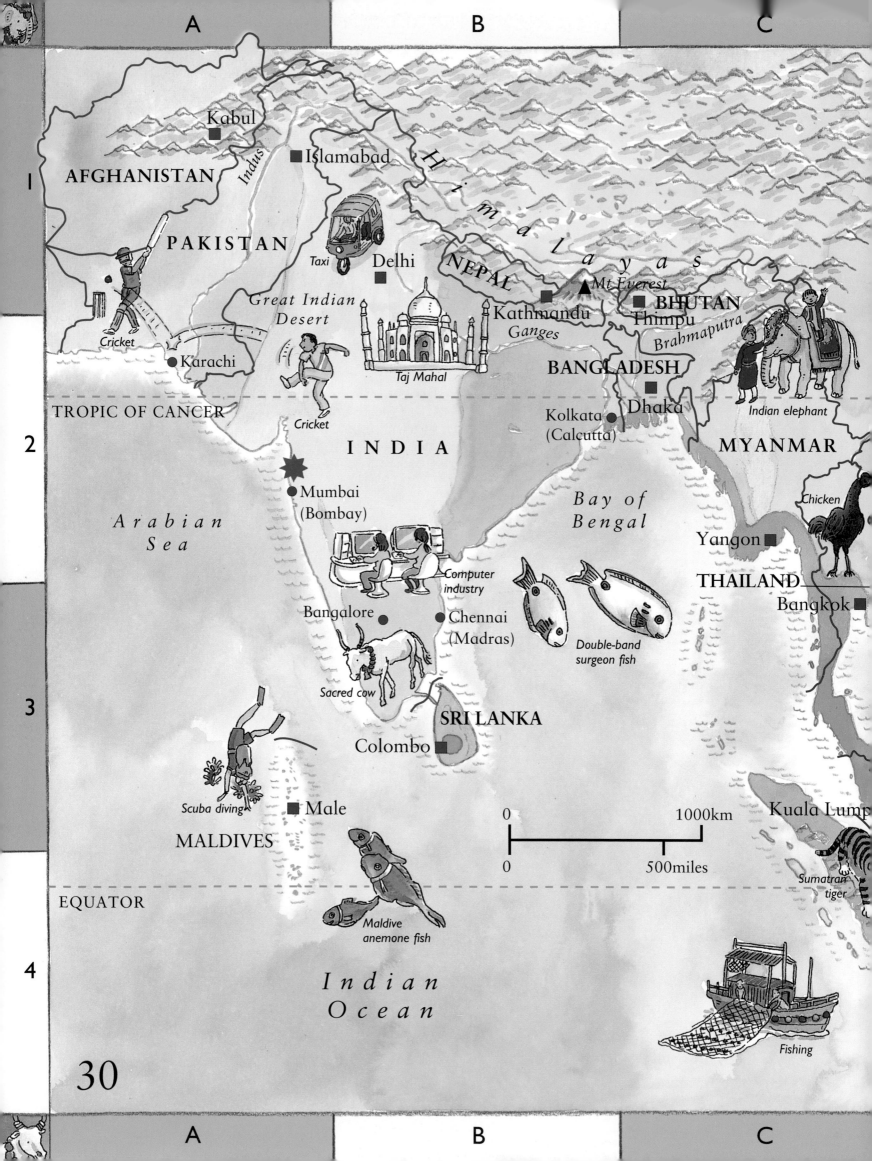

A

B

C

1

AFGHANISTAN

Kabul

Islamabad

Indus

PAKISTAN

Taxi

Delhi

NEPAL

H i m a l a y a s

▲ *Mt Everest*

BHUTAN

Thimpu

Cricket

Great Indian
Desert

Kathmandu

Ganges

Brahmaputra

Taj Mahal

BANGLADESH

Indian elephant

Karachi

Cricket

TROPIC OF CANCER

2

Kolkata
(Calcutta)

Dhaka

MYANMAR

I N D I A

*Bay of
Bengal*

Chicken

Mumbai
(Bombay)

*A r a b i a n
S e a*

*Computer
industry*

Yangon

THAILAND

Bangkok

Bangalore

Chennai
(Madras)

*Double-band
surgeon fish*

Sacred cow

SRI LANKA

3

Scuba diving

Colombo

Kuala Lumpu

0   1000km

Male

0   500miles

MALDIVES

*Sumatran
tiger*

EQUATOR

*Maldive
anemone fish*

4

*I n d i a n
O c e a n*

Fishing

30

A

B

C

Southern and southeastern Asia

The countries of this region are near the equator, so the weather is very hot. Dusty plains stretch across India. Thick rainforests grow in Malaysia and Indonesia. Most people farm in small villages, or work in big cities. A long mountain range called the Himalayas lies to the north.

VIETNAM
■ Hanoi

OS
entiane

Mekong

South China Sea

Basket boat

MBODIA

Rice

Phnom
Penh

Oil rig

■ Manila

PHILIPPINES

BRUNEI
Begawan Seri

ALAYSIA

SINGAPORE
ngapore

Orang utan

I N D O N E S I A

Rainforest

■ Jakarta

■ Dili
EAST TIMOR

The world's biggest movie industry, **Bollywood**, is based in Mumbai (Bombay), India. About 800 new films are made here every year.

Look for
the star ✸

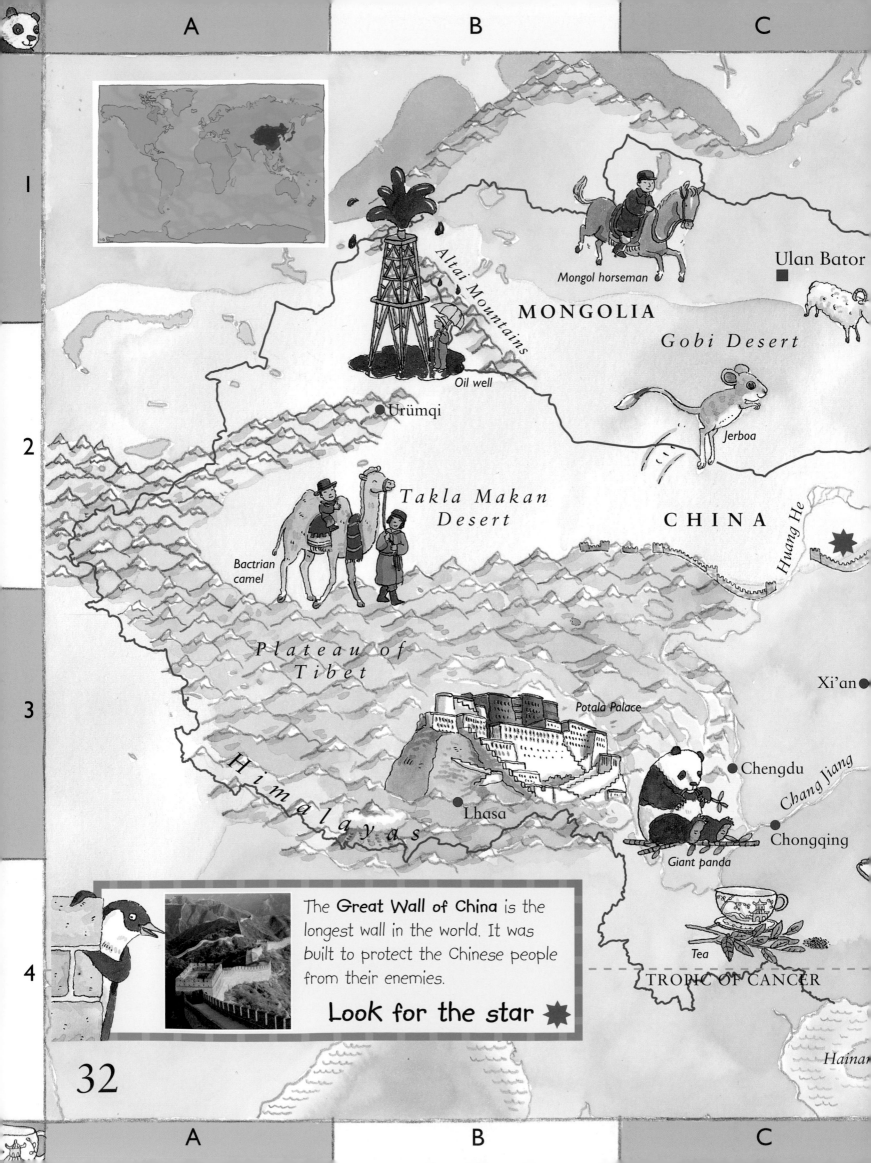

1

2

3

4

Altai Mountains

Oil well

MONGOLIA

Mongol horseman

Ulan Bator

Gobi Desert

Jerboa

Urümqi

Takla Makan Desert

CHINA

Bactrian camel

Huang He

Plateau of Tibet

Potala Palace

Xi'an

H i m a l a y a s

Chang Jiang

Giant panda

Chengdu

Lhasa

Chongqing

Tea

The **Great Wall of China** is the longest wall in the world. It was built to protect the Chinese people from their enemies.

Look for the star ✦

TROPIC OF CANCER

Hainan

0   1000km

0   500miles

1

Great Khingan Range

Sheep Farming

Harbin

Industry

The Forbidden City

Shenyang

2

Beijing

Tianjin

Pyongyang

NORTH KOREA

Seoul

Bulguksa temple

Sea of Japan

Squid

Honshu

Hokkaido

Bullet train

JAPAN

Terracotta warriors

SOUTH KOREA

Chinese junk

Himeji Castle

Mt Fuji

Tokyo

Nagoya

Osaka

Shikoku

East China Sea

Kyushu

Wuhan

Shanghai

3

China and Japan

More people live in China than anywhere else on earth. Most settle in the east, where they can farm the land or work in cities. To the north is Mongolia, and to the east are Korea, Taiwan and Japan. Japan is made up of many islands. Most Japanese people live on the four main islands, Hokkaido, Honshu, Shikoku and Kyushu, in very crowded cities.

Rice

Taipei

TAIWAN

Guangzhou

Hong Kong

4

South China Sea

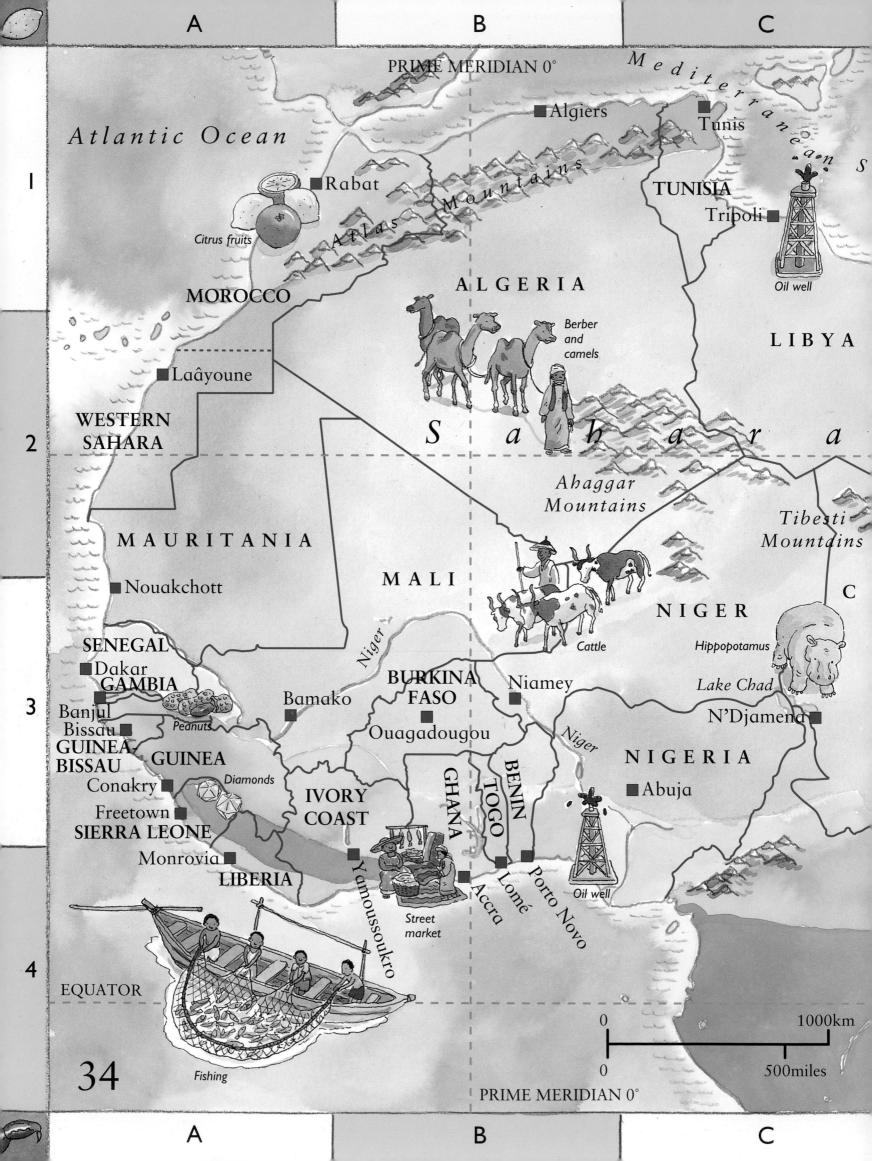

A

PRIME MERIDIAN 0°

Mediterranean s

Algiers

Tunis

Rabat

Citrus fruits

TUNISIA

Tripoli

Oil well

MOROCCO

A L G E R I A

Berber and camels

L I B Y A

WESTERN SAHARA

Laâyoune

S a h a r a

Ahaggar Mountains

Tibesti Mountains

M A U R I T A N I A

Nouakchott

M A L I

Cattle

N I G E R

Hippopotamus

Niger

SENEGAL

Dakar

GAMBIA

Banjul

Bissau

Peanuts

Bamako

BURKINA FASO

Niamey

Lake Chad

N'Djamena

Ouagadougou

GUINEA-BISSAU

GUINEA

Diamonds

NIGERIA

Abuja

Conakry

Freetown

IVORY COAST

GHANA

TOGO

BENIN

Oil well

SIERRA LEONE

Monrovia

LIBERIA

Yamoussoukro

Street market

Accra

Lomé

Porto Novo

EQUATOR

0 ——— 1000km

0 ——— 500miles

34

Fishing

PRIME MERIDIAN 0°

Atlantic Ocean

Atlas Mountains

C

Northern Africa

The Sahara is the world's biggest desert. It stretches across the whole of northern Africa. Most people live south of the Sahara or near the coast. The world's longest river, the Nile, flows from central Africa, through Egypt to the Mediterranean Sea.

TROPIC OF CANCER

Scorpion

EGYPT

Tutankhamun's funerary mask

Lake Nasser

Red Sea

■ Cairo

D

Cotton plant

Nile

Crocodile

S U D A N

■ Khartoum

ERITREA

■ Asmara

A S I A

DJIBOUTI

Ethiopian Highlands

■ Addis Ababa

E T H I O P I A

SOMALIA

■ Mogadishu

Starry triggerfish

Indian Ocean

The **pyramids**, near Cairo in Egypt, were built over 4,000 years ago. They are the largest stone buildings in the world.

Look for the star ✴

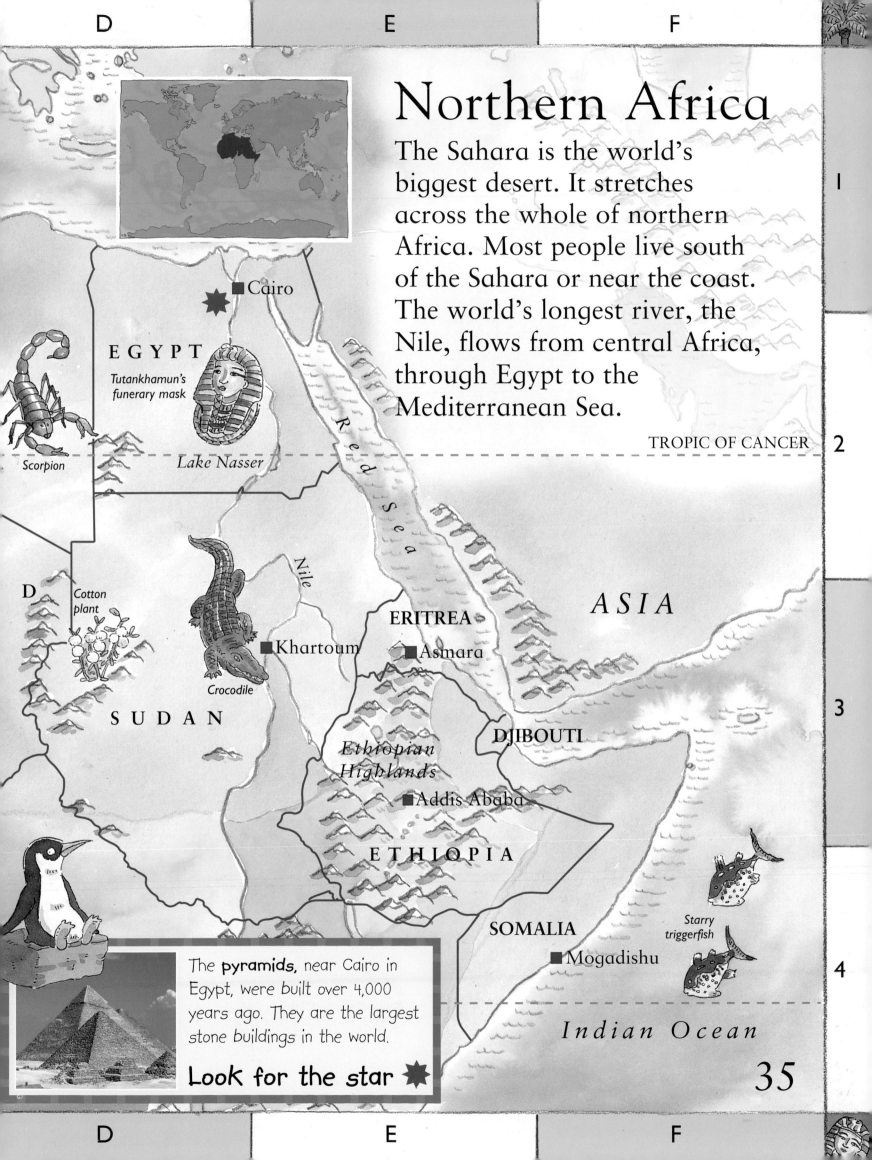

Southern Africa

Countries on the east coast of Africa, such as Kenya, are famous for the wildlife of the flat grasslands. Lions, elephants and giraffes all live in the savannah. To the west of Africa, the River Congo runs through thick rainforest. The huge Kalahari Desert is at the heart of southern Africa.

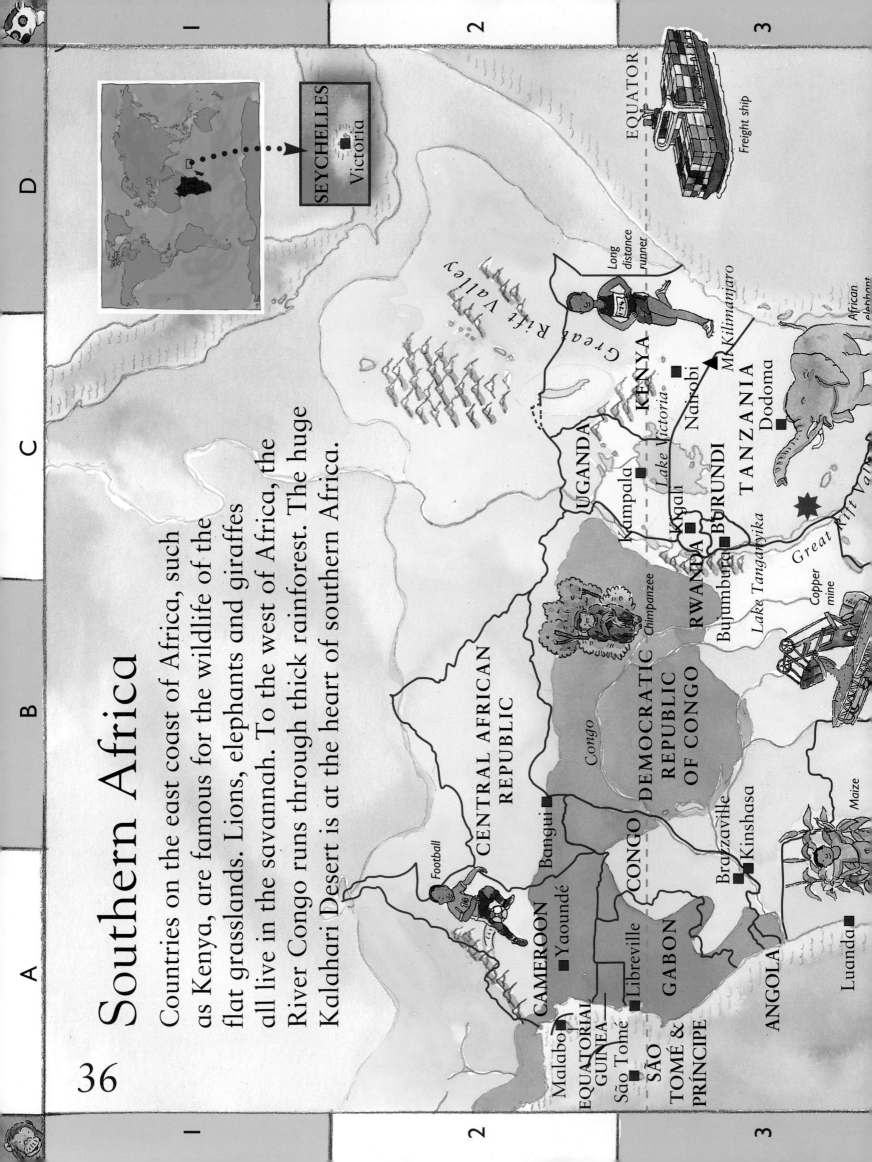

SEYCHELLES
Victoria

EQUATOR

Freight ship

Long distance runner

Great Rift Valley

UGANDA
Kampala

KENYA
Nairobi

Lake Victoria

RWANDA
Kigali

BURUNDI
Bujumbura

Mt Kilimanjaro

TANZANIA
Dodoma

Lake Tanganyika

African elephant

Copper mine

Great Rift Valley

Chimpanzee

CENTRAL AFRICAN REPUBLIC
Bangui

Congo

DEMOCRATIC REPUBLIC OF CONGO

CONGO
Brazzaville

Kinshasa

Maize

Football

CAMEROON
Yaoundé

EQUATORIAL GUINEA
Malabo

SÃO TOMÉ & PRÍNCIPE
São Tomé

GABON
Libreville

ANGOLA
Luanda

A   B   C   D

1   2   3

36

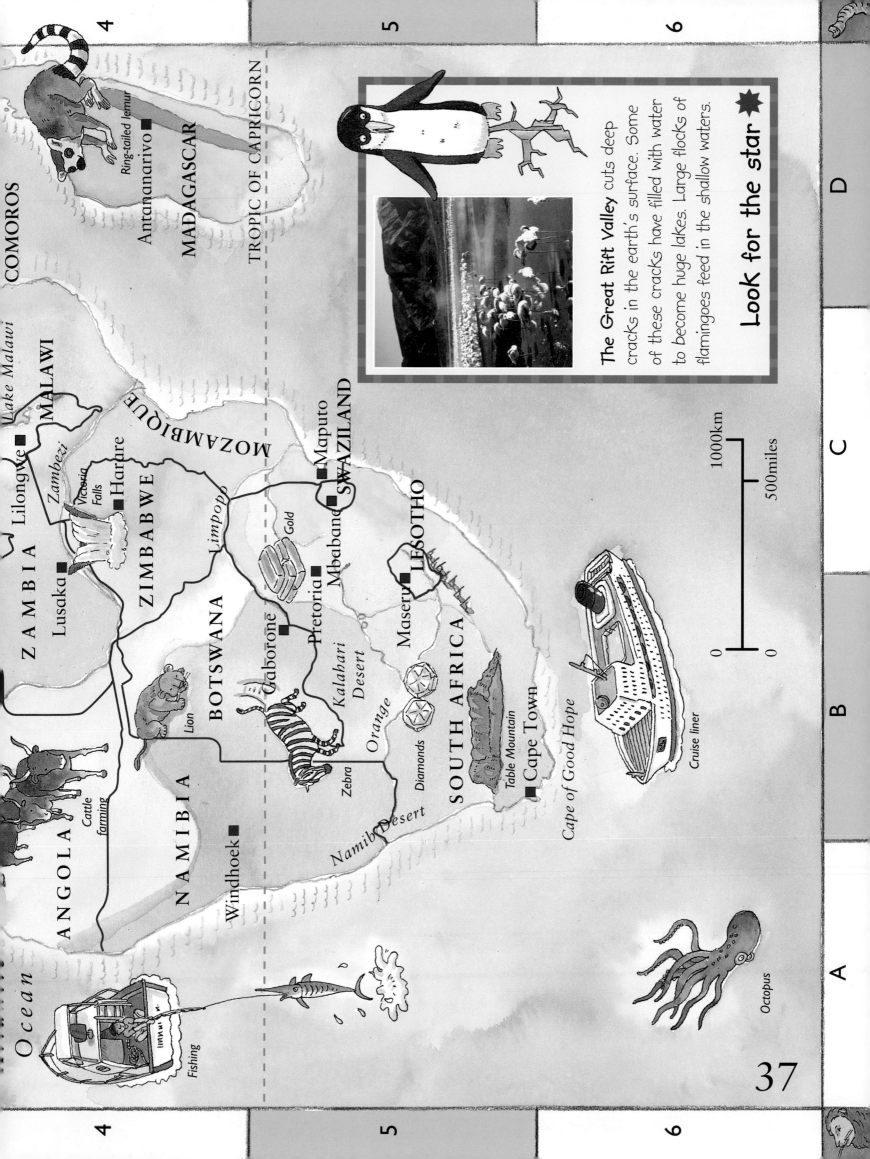

Ocean

COMOROS

MADAGASCAR

Ring-tailed lemur ■

Antananarivo

TROPIC OF CAPRICORN

Lake Malawi

MALAWI

Lilongwe ■

ZAMBIA

Lusaka ■

MOZAMBIQUE

Zambezi

Victoria Falls

Harare ■

ZIMBABWE

Maputo ■

SWAZILAND

Mbabane ■

Gold

Limpopo

Pretoria ■

LESOTHO

Maseru ■

Gaborone ■

BOTSWANA

Kalahari Desert

Orange

Diamonds

SOUTH AFRICA

Lion

Zebra

Cape Town ■

Table Mountain

NAMIBIA

Windhoek ■

Namib Desert

Cape of Good Hope

Cattle farming

ANGOLA

Fishing

Octopus

Cruise liner

Look for the star

The Great Rift Valley cuts deep cracks in the earth's surface. Some of these cracks have filled with water to become huge lakes. Large flocks of flamingoes feed in the shallow waters.

0   500miles
0   1000km

37

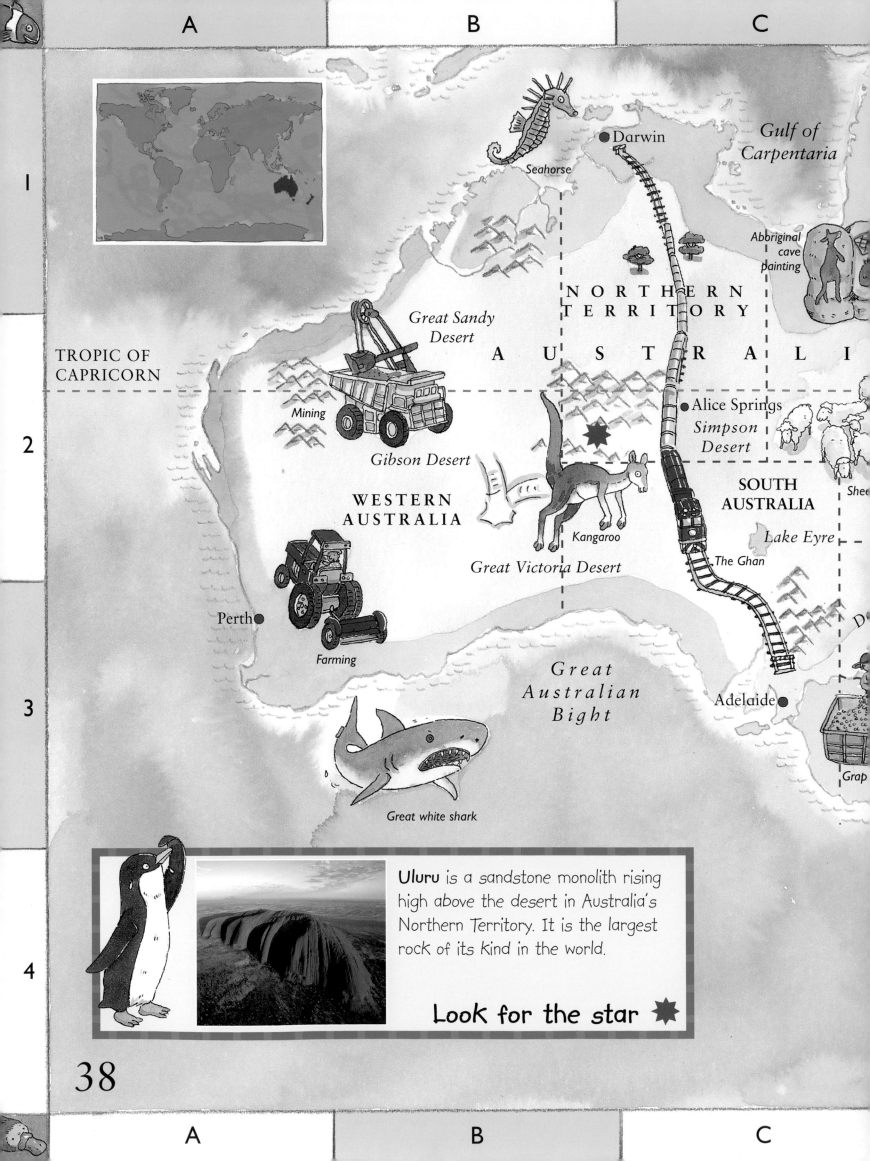

I

Seahorse

● Darwin

Gulf of Carpentaria

Aboriginal cave painting

TROPIC OF CAPRICORN

Great Sandy Desert

N O R T H E R N
T E R R I T O R Y

A U S T R A L I

Mining

2

Gibson Desert

● Alice Springs
Simpson Desert

WESTERN
AUSTRALIA

Kangaroo

SOUTH
AUSTRALIA

She

Lake Eyre

Great Victoria Desert

The Ghan

Perth ●

D

Farming

*Great
Australian
Bight*

3

Adelaide ●

Grap

Great white shark

Uluru is a sandstone monolith rising high above the desert in Australia's Northern Territory. It is the largest rock of its kind in the world.

4

Look for the star ✦

38

Australia and New Zealand

Australia is the only country that is also a continent. In the centre of Australia there are many deserts. To the north are tropical rainforests. Most Australian people live in cities by the sea.

New Zealand is 1,600km from Australia. It is a land of mountains and glaciers. Like Australia, it has many sheep and cattle farms.

Coral Sea

Clown fish

at Dividing Range

Barrier Reef

UEENSLAND

● Brisbane

Duck-billed platypus

NEW SOUTH WALES

Sydney ●

Sydney Opera House

urray

■ Canberra
AUSTRALIAN CAPITAL TERRITORY

TORIA

Melbourne ●

Surfing

ss Strait

Tasmanian devil

● Hobart

TASMANIA

Tasman Sea

Pacific Ocean

Red snapper fish

Rugby

NORTH ISLAND

NEW ZEALAND

● Auckland

● Hamilton

Lake Taupo

Kiwi

■ Wellington

SOUTH ISLAND

Mt Cook ▲

Southern Alps

● Christchurch

Fishing

● Dunedin

1000km

500miles

Yellow-fin fish

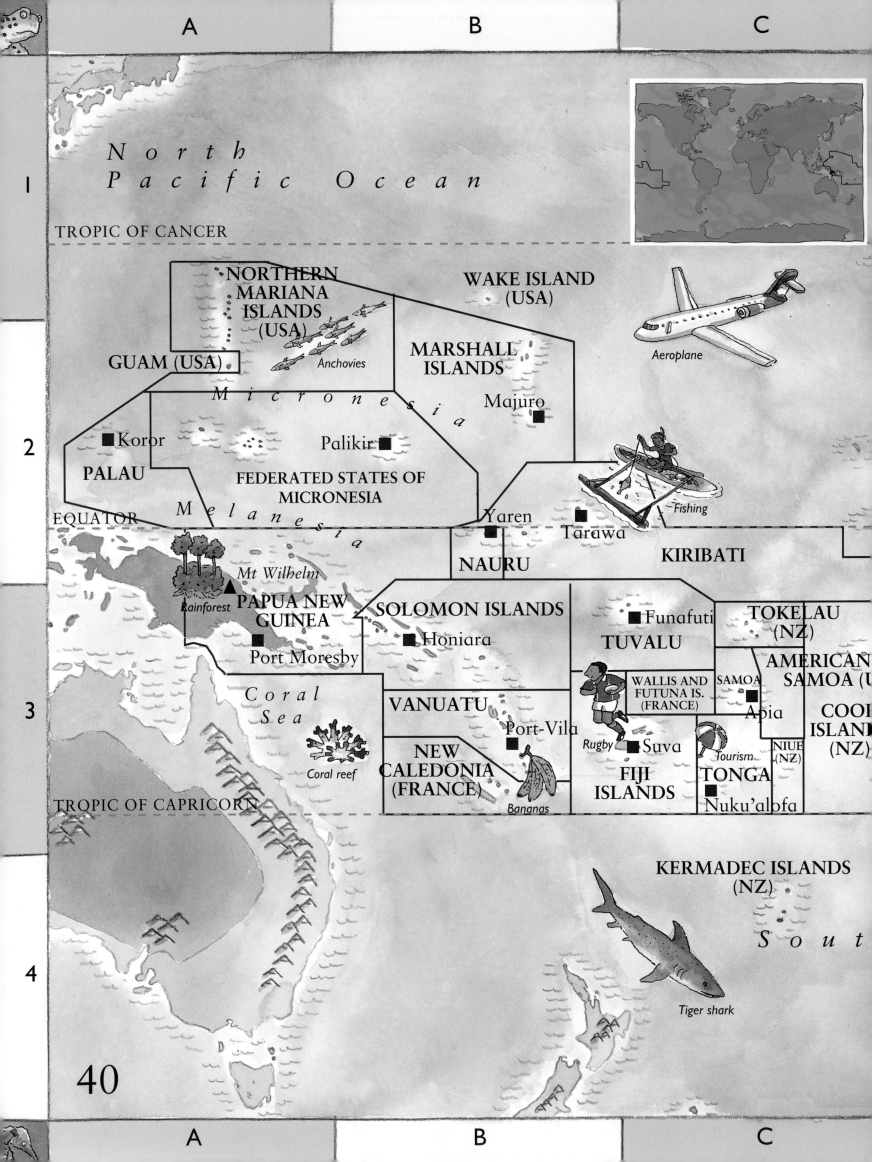

1

*North
Pacific Ocean*

TROPIC OF CANCER

**NORTHERN
MARIANA
ISLANDS
(USA)**

**WAKE ISLAND
(USA)**

GUAM (USA)

Anchovies

Aeroplane

**MARSHALL
ISLANDS**

M i c r o n e s i a

Majuro ■

2

■ Koror

Palikir ■

PALAU

**FEDERATED STATES OF
MICRONESIA**

M e l a n e s i a

EQUATOR

Yaren ■

Tarawa ■

Fishing

KIRIBATI

NAURU

Mt Wilhelm ▲

Rainforest

**PAPUA NEW
GUINEA**

SOLOMON ISLANDS

■ Funafuti

**TOKELAU
(NZ)**

TUVALU

**AMERICAN
SAMOA (U**

Honiara ■

Port Moresby ■

SAMOA ■

Apia

*Coral
Sea*

3

VANUATU

Port-Vila ■

WALLIS AND
FUTUNA IS.
(FRANCE)

Rugby

Suva ■

Tourism

NIUE
(NZ)

**COOI
ISLANI
(NZ)**

Coral reef

**NEW
CALEDONIA
(FRANCE)**

**FIJI
ISLANDS**

TONGA

Bananas

Nuku'alofa ■

TROPIC OF CAPRICORN

**KERMADEC ISLANDS
(NZ)**

S o u t

4

Tiger shark

40

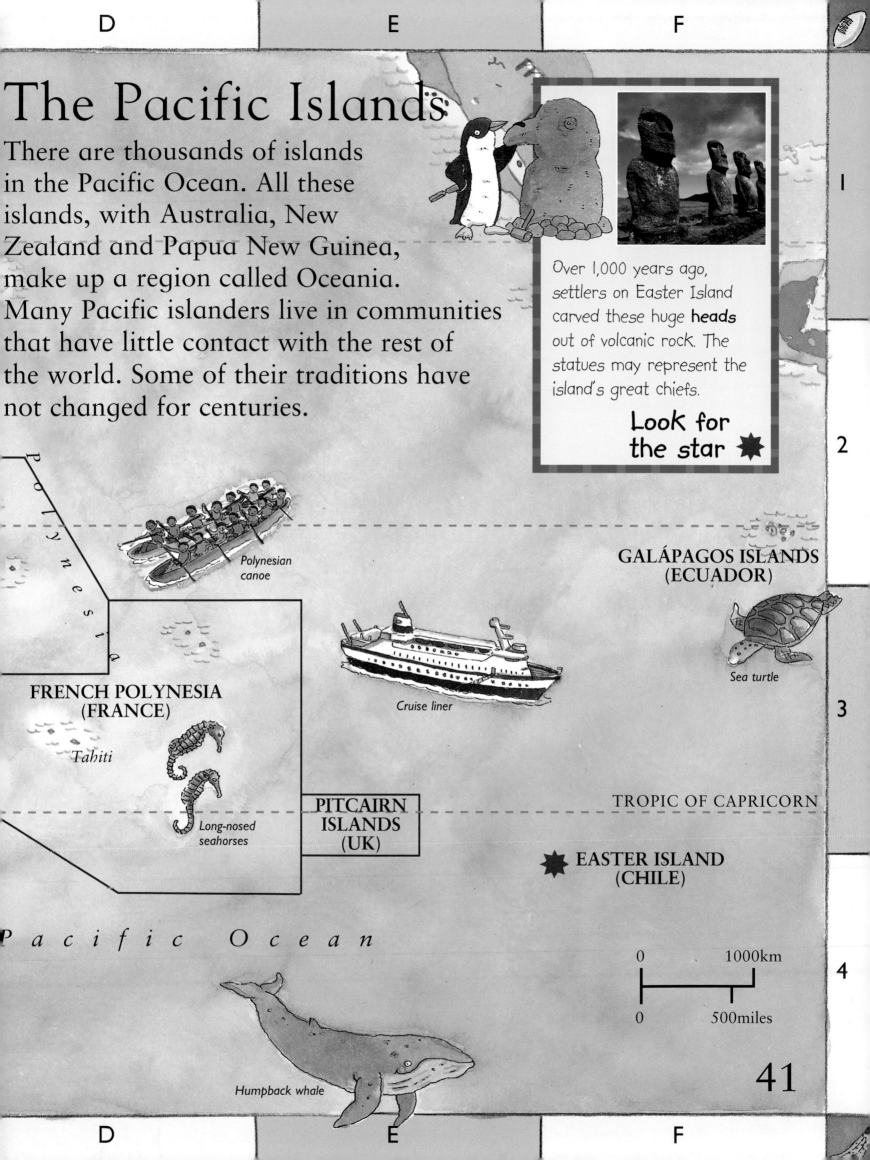

The Pacific Islands

There are thousands of islands in the Pacific Ocean. All these islands, with Australia, New Zealand and Papua New Guinea, make up a region called Oceania. Many Pacific islanders live in communities that have little contact with the rest of the world. Some of their traditions have not changed for centuries.

Over 1,000 years ago, settlers on Easter Island carved these huge **heads** out of volcanic rock. The statues may represent the island's great chiefs.

Look for the star ✴

Polynesian canoe

GALÁPAGOS ISLANDS (ECUADOR)

Sea turtle

FRENCH POLYNESIA (FRANCE)

Tahiti

Cruise liner

Long-nosed seahorses

PITCAIRN ISLANDS (UK)

TROPIC OF CAPRICORN

✴ EASTER ISLAND (CHILE)

P a c i f i c   O c e a n

Polynesia

0   1000km

0   500miles

41

Humpback whale

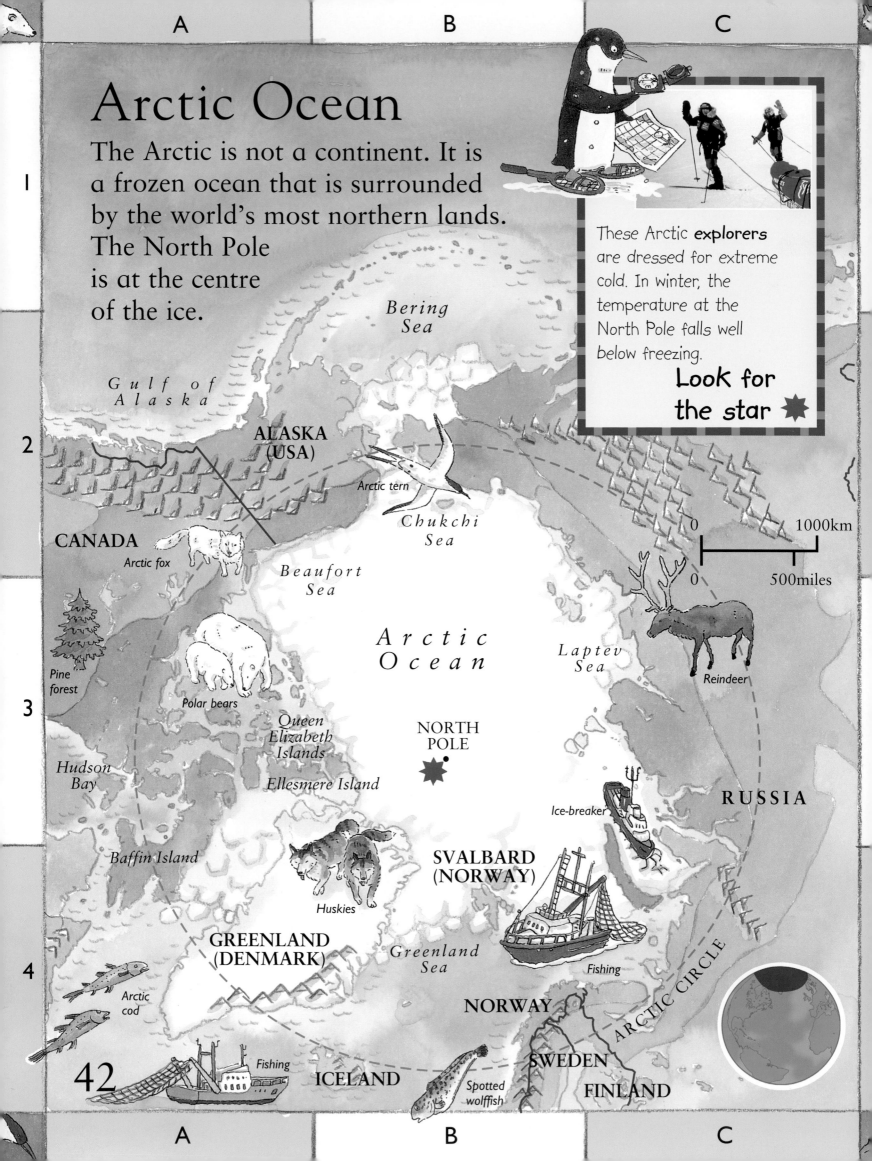

Arctic Ocean

The Arctic is not a continent. It is a frozen ocean that is surrounded by the world's most northern lands. The North Pole is at the centre of the ice.

These Arctic **explorers** are dressed for extreme cold. In winter, the temperature at the North Pole falls well below freezing.

Look for the star ✷

Bering Sea

Gulf of Alaska

ALASKA (USA)

Arctic tern

Chukchi Sea

Beaufort Sea

CANADA

Arctic fox

Pine forest

Polar bears

Arctic Ocean

Laptev Sea

Reindeer

0   1000km
0   500miles

Hudson Bay

Queen Elizabeth Islands

Ellesmere Island

NORTH POLE ✷

RUSSIA

Baffin Island

Ice-breaker

Huskies

SVALBARD (NORWAY)

GREENLAND (DENMARK)

Greenland Sea

Fishing

Arctic cod

NORWAY

ARCTIC CIRCLE

42

Fishing

ICELAND

Spotted wolffish

SWEDEN

FINLAND

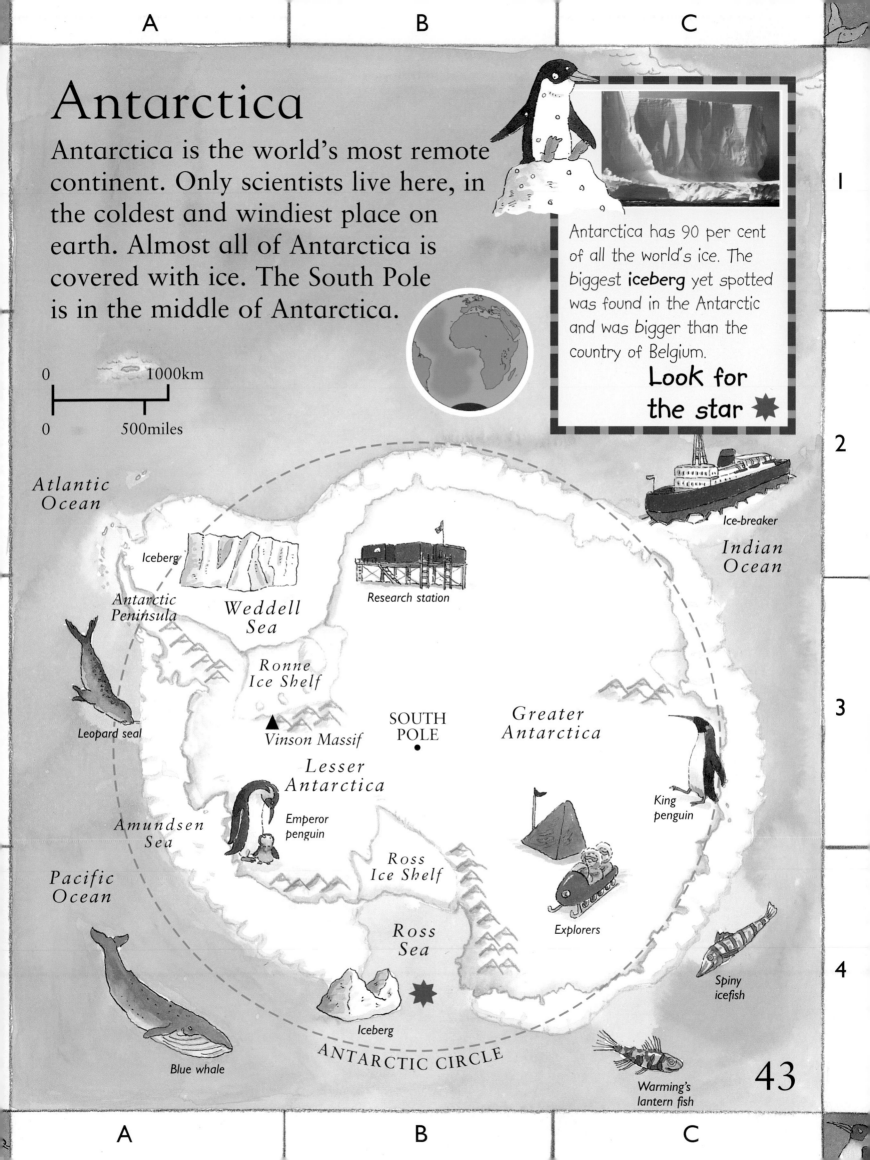

Antarctica

Antarctica is the world's most remote continent. Only scientists live here, in the coldest and windiest place on earth. Almost all of Antarctica is covered with ice. The South Pole is in the middle of Antarctica.

Antarctica has 90 per cent of all the world's ice. The biggest **iceberg** yet spotted was found in the Antarctic and was bigger than the country of Belgium.

Look for the star ✹

0   1000km

0   500miles

Atlantic Ocean

Iceberg

Antarctic Peninsula

Weddell Sea

Research station

Ice-breaker

Indian Ocean

Leopard seal

Ronne Ice Shelf

Vinson Massif

SOUTH POLE

Greater Antarctica

King penguin

Lesser Antarctica

Emperor penguin

Amundsen Sea

Pacific Ocean

Ross Ice Shelf

Explorers

Ross Sea

Spiny icefish

Iceberg

ANTARCTIC CIRCLE

Blue whale

Warming's lantern fish

43

1   ARCTIC CIRCLE

Fishing

Deep sea submersible

Car ferry

Blue whale

Cruise liner

2   TROPIC OF CANCER

Oil rig

Scuba diving

Caribbean Sea

Atlantic Ocean

Fishing

EQUATOR

Pacific Ocean

Freight ship

Fishing

TROPIC OF CAPRICORN

3

The oceans

Seen from space, the earth looks blue. This is because almost three quarters of the planet is covered with water. The earth has four great oceans, the Pacific, Atlantic, Indian and Arctic oceans. The Pacific is the biggest of these oceans.

Oil rig

Factory fishing ship

4

44

Iceberg

Arctic
Ocean

Ice-breaker

Mediterranean
Sea

Luxury yacht

Submarine

Pacific
Ocean

Chinese
junk

Arabian
Sea

Bay
of
Bengal

Fishing

Oil tanker

Coral
Sea

Indian
Ocean

Coral reef

Aeroplane

Racing
yacht

Oil rig

NTARCTIC
RCLE

Many **islands** are actually the peaks
of underwater mountains. Iceland is
the tip of one of the mountains of the
Mid-Atlantic Ridge.

Look for the star ✦

45

Index

46